To Mum and Dad
from David.

Fall 1986

The Polar Shelf

Dedication

To our wives, husbands, parents, children, friends . . .
to all who put up with the long absences of the people
involved with the Polar Continental Shelf Project . . .
we dedicate this book.

The Polar Shelf

The Saga of Canada's Arctic Scientists

By Michael Foster & Carol Marino

NC Press Limited Toronto 1986

Published by NC Press Limited *in cooperation with the Polar Continental Shelf Project, Energy Mines and Resources Canada and the Canadian Government Publishing Centre, Supply and Services Canada.*

Design, Lockwood Design Associates
Printing and Binding, Friesen Printers
Colour Separations, Graphitech Inc.
Typesetting, Kerr Graphics

We would like to thank the Ontario Arts Council and the Canada Council for their assistance in the production of this book.

Canadian Cataloguing in Publication Data
Marino, Carol, 1943-
   The Polar Shelf : the saga of Canada's Arctic scientists

ISBN 0-920053-63-7

1. Polar Continental Shelf Project (Canada)
2. Arctic research — Canada.   I. Foster, Michael, 1943-
II. Title.

QE48.C22A7 1986   557.19'9   C86-093626-0

New Canada Publications, a division of NC Press Limited,
Box 4010, Station A, Toronto, Ontario, Canada M5H 1H8

Printed and bound in Canada

Distributed in the United States of America by
Independent Publishers Group, One Pleasant Avenue, Port Washington,
New York 11050

Table of Contents

Acknowledgments

There have been many people who have quietly contributed their help in the creation of this book. Our thanks to Chris Bunting, Greta Greenhow, Marion Heintzman, Bonni Hrycyk, Morry Katz, Stephen MacPhee, Allison Mowat and Jackie Voyce.

Contributors: George Hobson — Director, Polar Continental Shelf Project, 1972 to the present; Fred Roots — Coordinator, Polar Continental Shelf Project, 1959 to 1971; W.E. van Steenburgh — Deputy Minister, Department of Mines and Technical Surveys, 1963 to 1966; Jim Harrison — Director of the Geological Survey of Canada, 1959 to 1964.

Frank Adams, technician; Fred Alt, base manager; Bill Anderson, oceanographer; Neil Anderson, hydrographer; R.J. Anderson, physical oceanographer; Jay Ardai, arctic engineer; Isa Asudeh, seismologist; Pierre Babusiaux, pilot; Susan Baker, chef, PCSP; Roger Belanger, photographer, Bedford Institute of Oceanography; George Benoit, technician; Harvey Blandford, hydrographer; Hewitt Bostock, geologist; Don Braun, pilot; Peter Bregg, photographer, Canapress; Robbie Burns, GSC technician; Bert Burry, pilot, airline owner and operator; George and Jim Burry, pilots; Eddy Chapman, base manager, PCSP; Arthur Collin, oceanographer; John Currie, helicopter pilot; Dick de Blicquy, pilot; Domenic Deluca, pilot; Jerry Dionne, pilot;

Ross Douglas, hydrographer; Harvey Easton, pilot; Michael Eaton, hydrographer; Sylvia Edlund, botanist; Roy Falconer, electronics engineer, Computing Devices of Canada; Norm Fenerty, photographer, Bedford Institute of Oceanography; Dave Forsyth, seismologist; Michael Foster, photographer; Horace Gardner, engineer; Axel Geiger, Geodetic Survey of Canada; David Gill, biologist; Chris Gorski, hydrographer; David Gray, animal behaviourist; Alan Heginbottom, geologist; Barry Hough, base manager, PCSP; Frank Hunt, topographical surveyor, field operations manager, PCSP; Ted Irving, geophysicist; Robert Iverson, U.S. Army Map Service; Ruth Jackson, geophysicist; John Jacobsen, contractor, Arctic Resources; Peter Jacobsen, contractor, Arctic Resources; Linda Jefferson, graduate student in archeology; Peter Jones, chemical oceanographer; Mike Kelly, photographer; Adam Kerr, hydrographer; Roy Koerner, glaciologist; Al Koudys, hydrographer; Joe Kreke, helicopter pilot-engineer; Tom Krochak, chef, PCSP; Pierre Lamothe, animal behaviourist; Valery Lee, oceanographer; Robert Lillestrand, U.S. space navigation specialist; Lausanne Losier, hydrographer; Leif Lundgaard, technician, PCSP; Hugh MacAuley, GSC technician; Stu MacDonald, animal behaviourist; Joe MacInnis, underwater researcher; Peter MacKinnon, glaciologist; Brian MacLean, geologist; Doug McLeod, pilot; Robert McGhee, archeologist; Peter Osborne, technician, PCSP;

Peary caribou, 1973. (photographer: David Gray)

The herd of caribou came to me — all I had to do was sit there and be quiet. That was the last opportunity to see caribou in that way, because that winter they all died on Bathurst Island. The caribou have started coming back from that great die-off in 1974. And still the recovery is not that great.
— David Gray

Tony Overton, seismologist; W.S.B. Paterson, glaciologist; Mike Pearlman, Ocean Research Corporation, U.S.; Bernard Pelletier, geologist; Bill Presley, base mechanic, PCSP; Dave Pugh, hydrographer; Hans Pulkkinen, hydrographer; Peter Reshitnyk, scientific technician; Rick Riewe, biologist; Richard Rondeau, helicopter mechanic; Charlie Roots, technician, PCSP; Dale Russell, graduate student in archeology; Denis St-Onge, geologist; Bob Schieman, electronics technician; Al Singh, helicopter engineer; Brian Smiley, bio-oceanographer; Donald Smith, gravity observer; Larry Sobczak, geophysicist; Randy Stevenson, geophysicist; Pat Sutherland, archeologist; George Sutton, artist; Jack Sweeney, geophysicist; Phillip Taylor, ornithologist; William Tyrlik, seismologist; Dorothy Van Eyk, botanist; Gus Vilks, geologist; Jean-Serge Vincent, geologist; Hans Weber, geophysicist; Peter Wilson, Decca station manager, now president of Surnav.

PCSP STAFF, 1985: Bea Alt, Chris Barmig, Jocelyne Bourgeois, Ed Chapman, Barry Fagan, Bob Fardais, Ed Feldman, David Fisher, Jim Godden, Emile Gravelle, Margaret Herzog, George Hobson, Barry Hough, Frank Hunt, Roy Koerner, Jacques Lepage, Marcia McKay, Murty Parnandi, Bill Presley, Harry Scott, Giselle Simard, Jackie Voyce.

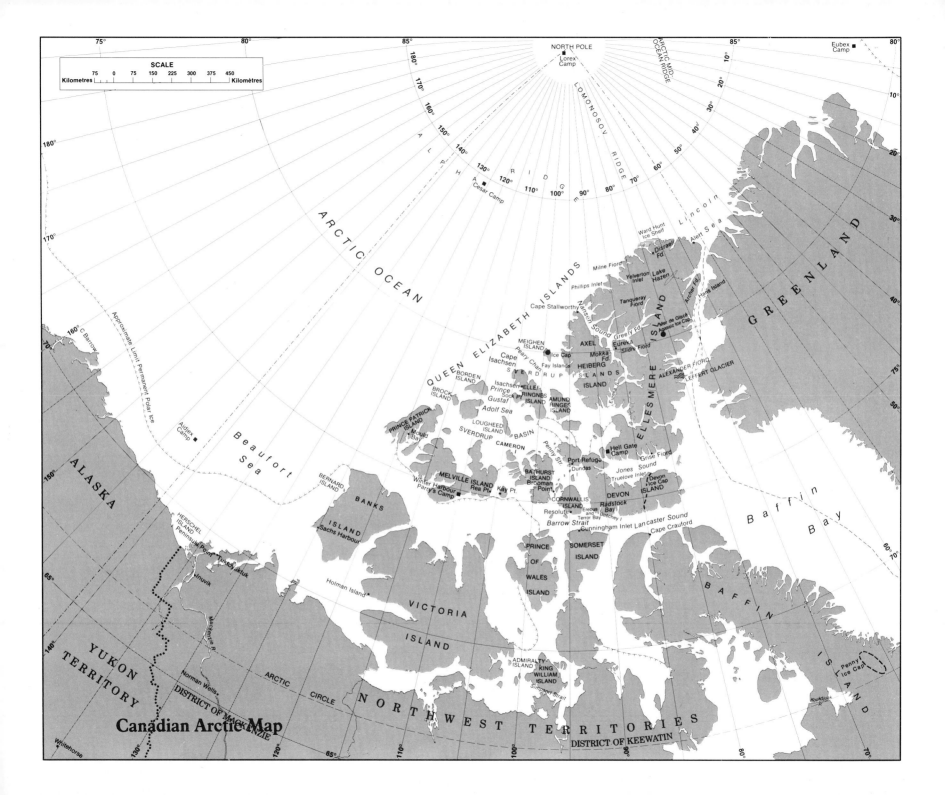

Canadian Arctic Map

Foreword

On April 5, 1958 the Government of Canada created the Polar Continental Shelf Project. Its purpose was to conduct scientific research and strengthen Canada's sovereignty in the Far North. In 1960 the PCSP mounted its first full-scale, systematic survey and research program.

At the time, most Canadians were unaware that the Project had been formed. Twenty-five years later, despite an impressive record of achievement by the Project, few Canadians outside government and scientific circles are aware of what happens north of the 70th parallel. The work has been done, and is being done, quietly, efficiently and economically, by people who are dedicated to the pursuit of their science, not to publicity.

This book celebrates the 25th anniversary of the Polar Continental Shelf Project's first field season and honours the work of a small and dedicated group which has achieved much.

It is a story worth telling.

A helicopter flies off Prince of Wales Island on a hydrographic survey in 1981. (photographer: Michael Foster)

> *We had a little sleigh we could put together in about 15 minutes. To get the helicopters started, we'd take the batteries out, put them on the sleigh and pull them in to where it was warm. If the helicopters had synthetic oil, it'd be just like molasses if you left it out overnight. So we'd drain that, put it on the sleigh, and haul it to where it was warm, too.*
> *— Harvey Easton*

Background

"The idea of Polar Shelf had been around in the late 40s and 50s. The launch of *Sputnik* in 1957 pushed the Canadian government for a presence in the Arctic. Then the Americans wanted to put one up. Well, you need to know the effect of gravity to put a satellite up. They came to us and asked if we would supply the data on gravity in the Arctic, or if not, they would go up there and get it themselves. We decided it would be better if we supplied the data.

"At the same time, the Law of the Sea Conference gave all countries dominion over their own continental shelf, and we realized that ours had never been explored or mapped. We knew nothing about it except what the Russians and Americans could tell us."
— *George Hobson*
Director, Polar Continental Shelf Project

To understand the work of the Polar Continental Shelf Project, one has to look a little further back in history. During World War II, northern Canada had become an area of great interest to military, political and scientific leaders. The United States had built airbases at Goose Bay and Frobisher Bay to ferry aircraft across Greenland to Europe. More airbases were built at Whitehorse and Norman Wells to support the construction of the Alaska Highway and the Canol Pipeline.

Up to that time, little had been known about the problems of arctic aviation, polar navigation and meteorological forecasting in polar regions. However, a great deal was learned from wartime experience — especially in weather forecasting. The information that came out of these bases proved to be so useful in forecasting weather in North America that Canada and the United States agreed to build jointly five weather stations in the Queen Elizabeth Islands. Between 1947 and 1950 they built Eureka and Alert on Ellesmere Island, Resolute on Cornwallis Island, Isachsen on Ellef Ringnes Island and Mould Bay on Prince Patrick Island.

Common defence requirements increased the presence and involvement of the United States in Canada's north. In 1951 Canada and the United States built the Pinetree Line, thirty-nine radar stations along the 50th parallel. The Mid-Canada Line, on the 55th parallel, followed in 1954 and the next year, the Distant Early Warning Line (the DEW Line) along the 70th parallel. In 1957 the two countries formed the North American Air Defence Command.

This intensification of activity in the North brought increasing demand for scientific and technical information and for improved techniques of construction and transportation. For the first time, Canadian government agencies had to respond to foreign requests for information about the North. And often that information was simply not available.

Mokka Fiord, Axel Heiberg Island. (photographer: Stu MacDonald)

One of the first steps Canada took to meet this need for information was Operation Franklin in 1955, which was organized by Yves Fortier and Ray Thorsteinsson of the Geological Survey of Canada. It was a twenty-eight-person expedition including scientists from many disciplines. By pooling their research budgets they were able to use two long-range Sikorsky S-55 helicopters to fly field parties from four main base camps 320 km apart. In a single season, they mapped and studied strategic locations over 258 998.8 square kilometres on Somerset, Prince of Wales, Melville, Cornwallis, Bathurst, Devon, Ellesmere, Axel Heiberg, Amund Ringnes and Ellef Ringnes islands.

There were two major benefits from Operation Franklin. Scientific data showed a very thick accumulation of sedimentary rocks and structures similar to those found in oil fields. The petroleum industry quickly responded by applying for permits to explore these structures in more detail. The other benefit was experience. Operation Franklin demonstrated how productive joint research using modern technology could be, and provided the first lessons in complex logistical planning.

"We made the jump from dog team and canoe to helicopters, and I happened to be the guy in charge of logistics. Operation Franklin gave us our first experience in accommodating the requirements of fieldwork to the rather different requirements of working with sophisticated mechanical transports."
— Fred Roots
First director of the Polar
Continental Shelf Project

Fred Roots, PCSP director, 1959. (photographer: Bert Burry)

You take Fred Roots. He's a geologist, but what is his area of knowledge? He had tremendous knowledge about helicopters, about fuel and gas caches, and the economics of getting somewhere. He's an expert working with dogs and with Ski-Doos, and he knows all of those logistics because when he was a field man, he had to learn all those other things besides geology to get the information he wanted.
— *Neil Anderson*

This gyrfalcon aerie on Ellesmere was made entirely of bones of arctic hares. The nest was several feet thick and presumably very old. The bones were cemented together with whitewash from the chicks. Ordinarily gyrfalcons lay their eggs right on a bare ledge or occupy a nest made by some other species.
— *Stu MacDonald*

Gyrfalcons at their nest. (photographer: Stu MacDonald)

In 1957 the pressure for information about the North increased dramatically when the Soviet Union launched *Sputnik*, the first satellite. In 1958 the U.S. nuclear-powered submarine *Nautilus* made the first under-ice crossing of the Arctic Ocean. That same year, the International Conference on the Law of the Sea gave nations the rights to mineral and other resources on their continental shelves as far as 200 miles off shore. Canada was now claiming ownership of resources on a polar continental shelf about which we knew virtually nothing. The only information we had, other than that gleaned during Operation Franklin, was based on studies made during the Canadian Arctic Expedition of 1913-18, led by Vilhjalmur Stefansson, and on maps published in the United States and the Soviet Union.

All that was about to change.

On March 10, 1958, W.E. van Steenburgh, Director General of Scientific Surveys for the Department of Mines and Technical Surveys (now the Department of Energy, Mines and Resources), and later Deputy Minister of the department, presided at a special meeting of the Technical Sub-Committee of the Advisory Committee on Northern Development. Attending were representatives from the Dominion Observatory (now part of the Geological Survey of Canada), the Hydrographic Service, the Geological Survey of Canada and the Geographical Branch of the Department of Mines and Technical Surveys; the Defence Research Board; the National Research Council; the Department of Northern Affairs and National Resources

(now Indian and Northern Affairs); the Fisheries Research Board (now part of Fisheries and Oceans); and other interested government agencies. Considerable advance work on the problems to be discussed had been done by Fred Roots and his associates at Mines and Technical Surveys so that the subcommittee could take action. They recommended that a new organization, the Polar Continental Shelf Project (PCSP), be formed:

"PCSP will aim at hydrographic, oceanographic, geophysical and biological studies of the entire Canadian Polar Continental Shelf and, if it is so desired later, the Canadian Arctic Basin. The area of interest for the initial season will be a band 200 miles long, centred on Isachsen and stretching 200 miles out to sea.... The Project will ultimately embrace the entire Arctic Continental Shelf."

The subcommittee proposed the establishment of permanent scientific, magnetic and tidal stations at four of the Joint Arctic Weather Stations (JAWS): Isachsen, Alert, Mould Bay and Resolute. It recommended taking gravity, geomagnetic, oceanographic and hydrographic observations at regular intervals; geological studies of surficial sediments and tracings of bedrock provinces; study of the distribution and movement of ice, terrain conditions, soil processes and permafrost; and research on marine animals and fishes. The subcommittee wanted PCSP to be in the field in 1959 and recommended that heavy equipment be shipped by sea to Resolute during the summer of 1958. The budget for the 1958-59 season was established at $266 000, of which $150 000 was allocated to a sophisticated electronic navigational system. One month later the recommendations were submitted to Cabinet. On April 5, 1958 the Polar Continental Shelf Project was established by Cabinet directive. Things were moving — and very quickly.

Off Rae Point in 1981, the Coast Guard ship Louis St. Laurent *tries to guide the supply ship* Arctic Tide *into Rae Point through the autumn ice. Not until this stop has been made can both ships go on to Resolute Bay to unload Polar Shelf's supplies for the next season. Only then can Polar Shelf personnel go south for the winter. (photographer: Michael Foster)*

15

"Cabinet was convinced that the far northern islands could become a great national asset, that Canada needed a more definitive presence in the islands and that perhaps scientific exploration as a national policy was the logical way to achieve this sovereignty."
— *George Hobson*

The Project now existed on paper — but only on paper. Aside from the enormous amount of logistical work to be done for the following summer's field trip, PCSP as yet had no director, no operation procedures, no staff, and no firm strategy for fulfilling its mandate.

Fred Roots spent the summer of 1958 winding up Operation Stikine in northwestern British Columbia. At the end of the summer, two senior men from the Geological Survey of Canada, Jim Harrison and Hewitt Bostock, came to inspect the work.

"We sat down on some boulders and fell to talking about the best ways to conduct future earth science studies. We began to sketch out what we would do if we had a free hand. The established agencies, with long traditions, were finding it hard to work together, so we seriously considered starting all over again. By the end of the afternoon, the germs of some ideas were planted in the minds of these senior scientists."
— *Fred Roots*

That autumn, Roots was summoned back to Ottawa and offered the job of directing the kind of agency he and his associates had been talking about for years: the Polar Continental Shelf Project.

"We planned our new group directly under van Steenburgh. And we had strong support from all the other agencies — provided we didn't take too many resources from them, of course.

"We knew we had to have a strong survey-control team. I was insistent from the beginning that whatever we did would not be reconnaissance for its own sake: the work we were going to do in the High Arctic should be of the same scientific quality and accuracy as work done anywhere else, regardless of latitude. And, to a given scale, we should do things only once. We should go as slowly as necessary, as modestly as necessary, but we should do our work well, from the beginning. The Project grew, almost inevitably, from 1946 to 1958. All of us, looking back, could see it coming. PCSP is the result of all sorts of people's work. We really had to struggle to make it happen, but it was an idea whose time had come. We could make a case for it from nearly every point of view: it was cheaper to work together than in separate expeditions; it fitted into the politics of the time — and it still does; it brought Canada, an Arctic-rim nation, into the forefront of Arctic research; and we profited from steadily growing interest in the resources of the Arctic Islands and the Polar Continental Shelf. Best of all, we had fun! Enthusiasm for this new venture came from the very top, and all of us in the field felt a strong sense of quiet excitement."
— *Fred Roots*

Arctic fox pups play on Bathurst Island, 1977
(photographer: David Gray)

Eddy Chapman, Tuktoyaktuk base manager, at the settlement of Holman Island on Victoria Island in 1978. (photographer: George Hobson)

"These days, people fresh out of university who want some information from the Arctic are just magically transported out there. Without Polar Shelf, they would have to learn what it means to get money for helicopters, to run a logistics operation, learn all that has to be done to get there and back out again in order to get a crucial bit of information."

— *Neil Anderson*
Hydrographer

The organization of the Polar Continental Shelf Project has changed little since day one. The Project is set up as a small unit of the Department of Energy Mines and Resources (formerly Mines and Technical Surveys). Financial support comes from a special fund granted annually by Parliament. The Project team is responsible to the department's Assistant Deputy Minister of Earth Sciences, and works in direct cooperation with the two main field survey branches: the Geological Survey of Canada, and Surveys and Mapping, as well as other government agencies and nongovernment organizations engaged in Arctic field work.

Whenever practicable, studies are carried out by the agency responsible or specializing in a particular subject. Polar Shelf provides the logistical support, field facilities and equipment. Studies not directed by other agencies are organized as activities of the Project itself. Polar Shelf therefore acts as the instigator and executor of independent field research programs and also supports the activities of other agencies that would not otherwise be able to undertake such work in the Arctic. Between these two roles are many gradations. This flexibility keeps the scientific and technical responsibility in the hands of those most qualified.

"It's been a very creative government activity. The core logistical service that was set up supported a wide, diverse set of activities. The broad concept of putting together an organization — a very small number of people who had an attitude of making it happen in the Arctic — really does work. Everything is focused towards supporting the field parties. With a very small staff in Ottawa, a very large operation is being directed in the Arctic."

— *Neil Anderson*

We were the oddballs one winter, a camp of two people in Polar Bear Pass on Bathurst Island. The Polar Shelf staff had gone south for the winter, so we became Polar Shelf. Our call sign was Polar Shelf Bathurst. For us, hearing base manager Eddy Chapman back on the radio again for Polar Shelf was really a highlight marking the end of the winter. We were back in Polar Shelf's hands. — David Gray

A traditional Inuit sled and team at Mould Bay, 1963.
(photographer: Harvey Easton)

Finding the Way

When the Polar Continental Shelf Project was established, its terms of reference were very wide. This was deliberate because there was so much to learn and such a large area to investigate. The area, running from Alaska to Greenland, is a band about 640 km deep that extends 160 km into the Arctic Ocean and 483 km south into the Archipelago from the ocean front.

One of the first problems was to decide on the scope and scale of the program. At the beginning, emphasis was given to oceanography, hydrography, various aspects of geophysics, and submarine geology. PCSP staff were determined to produce results that were of the same standard and accuracy as those achieved in other parts of the country. But they had yet to face the special problems of doing scientific research in the Far North.

They realized very quickly that navigation was a major hurdle. They had to find a way of fixing almost instantly the position of the scientific and survey stations, up to 320 km from the

Supplies are brought into a camp at Tanquaray Fiord, Ellesmere Island, 1978. (photographer: Peter Reshitnyk)

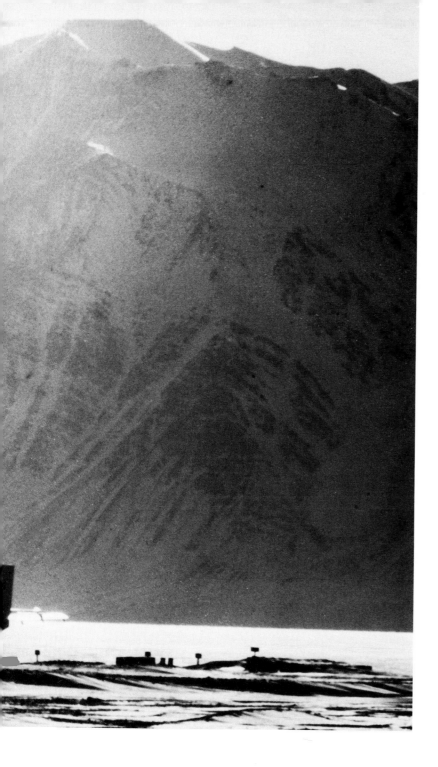

At Isachsen in 1959, dog sled runners are being greased with Cream of Wheat. A Decca receiver is mounted on the sled. (photographer: Roy Falconer)

nearest fixed-reference point, across shifting ice and under continuous low overcast. The position-finding method had to allow other parties to return to the same location, regardless of changing ice conditions or movement of the ice pack. It had to provide coordinates others could use, so that help and supplies could be delivered in emergencies.

Besides having the required range and accuracy, the navigational system had to be portable enough to be installed by small aircraft, and be capable of giving positions while in a moving aircraft, helicopter, snowmobile or dog sled, or while fixed or drifting erratically. It had to provide positions to any number of field parties at the same time and it had to be affected as little as possible by the aurora, by low sun altitude, and by the change of general conductivity caused by the disappearance of snow from the land and sea ice and by surface melting.

These prerequisites called for an electronic system, but no standard electronic-survey system then on the market was suitable.

Polar Shelf staff decided that little would be gained from broad reconnaissances across the whole continental shelf area. Surveys and research would be confined to specific areas, which they would study in detail before moving on. The Arctic Ocean front was divided into a series of blocks, each about 320 km by 480 km to 640 km. In any one season, the main work of the Project would be concentrated in one of the blocks. The first block to be studied was centred at Isachsen on Ellef Ringnes Island.

The organization of the Project began in earnest in November 1958, and the first field party was due to leave for the Arctic in early March 1959. That first season was designed primarily to evaluate techniques and answer questions.

First, they had to know the conditions under which the electronic position-finding system would have to operate. They had to find out what was the best time and practical length of the field season for each of the various studies. They had to determine which activities could be combined, to save aircraft support and duplication of camps. What was the expected pace of each activity and how much could be done in each season? Which studies could be best done from a central base and which

required mobile field camps? What were the transport requirements, from freighter aircraft to dog teams, and what were the internal and external communication needs?

On March 9, 1959 the first field party set off in search of some answers to these questions. Professional staff of the first party included Director Fred Roots, hydrographer Harvey Blandford, surveyor Frank Hunt, hydrographer Adam Kerr, gravity observer Donald Smith, oceanographer Bill Anderson, and hydrographer Michael Eaton. By March 14 the entire team, including support personnel, two aircraft, a Beaver and an Otter, as well as seven tonnes of equipment had been delivered to Resolute. The next day, six of them took the Otter and flew on to the Joint Arctic Weather Station at Isachsen. That would be 'home' until mid-October.

They got to work quickly. Even as more equipment and supplies were being shuttled in from Resolute, they began to run a 300 km survey line from a geodetic point near Isachsen, across the ice of the Prince Gustaf Adolf Sea and Peary Channel to Borden Island to the west and

At Isachsen, a flame gun is used to dig holes for anchoring the guy wires of Decca towers — an experiment not repeated. (photographer: Roy Falconer)

A 1960 PCSP team prepare to evacuate their camp on the Arctic Ocean because of the pressure ridge build-up. (photographer: George Hobson)

Melville Island, 1963. Glaciologist Stan Paterson is on the left, Frank Hunt on the right. (photographer: Harvey Easton)

The tellurometer station north of Cape Isachsen.
(photographer: Fred Roots)

Meighen Island to the northeast. This line would be the base line for the future electronic network that was so important to the success of the Project.

"When I was choosing whom to take, it took me about six seconds to suggest the one I wanted first ... and I wanted Frank Hunt. He was far and away the most experienced winter topographical surveyor we had at that time. He had run the 60th parallel survey in wintertime. He had already shown that just because it is cold and the wind is blowing, there is no reason to be less accurate with a theodolite than when it is nice and sunny. He's still with PCSP."
— *Fred Roots*

Frank Hunt ran the survey line with tellurometer (an electronic distance-measuring instrument) and theodolite (an instrument for measuring angles), using stations on high points of pressure ridges on the pack ice. At temperatures of –40°C, or colder, a new technique had to be devised to make the tellurometer work. The transmitting head was positioned over the station, while the body of the instrument was housed in a heated tent, no more than 4.5 m away. Reaching this tent, so close to the highest

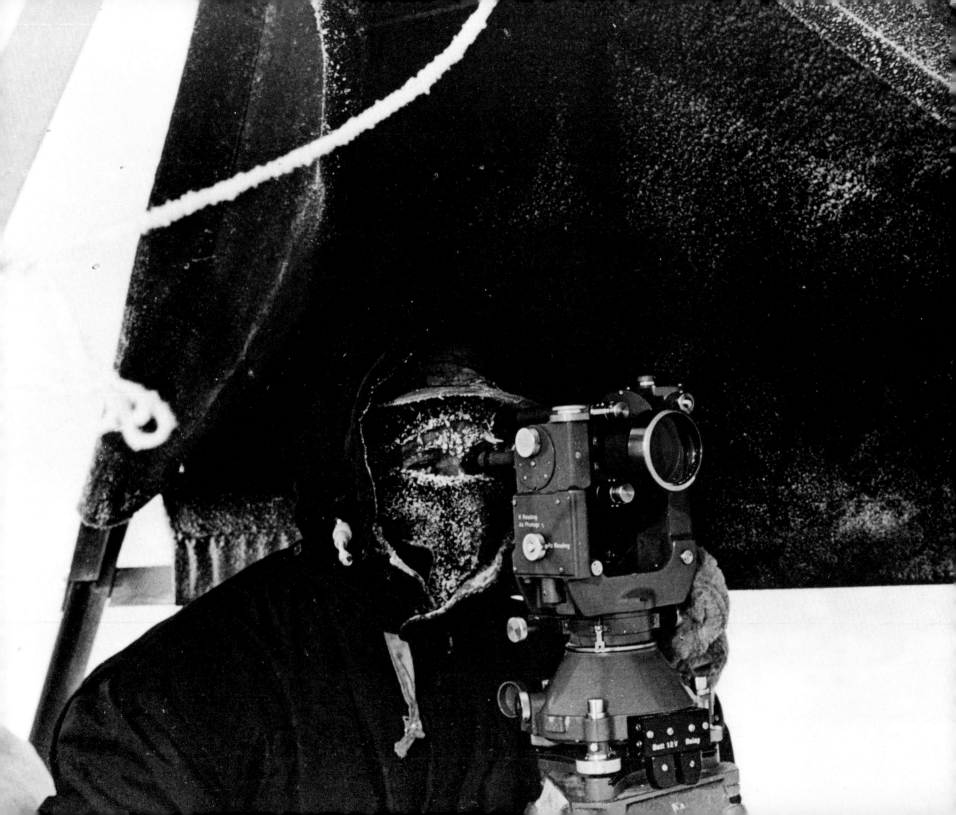

point around, was often difficult, requiring ice-climbing techniques.

By the first week of April the survey line had reached Borden Island and the team had made its first oceanographic station on the frozen Prince Gustaf Adolf Sea. Several days later, they got the first successful bottom sample from the ocean floor 434 m below. Oceanographic work was confined to two stations — both out in the open, at temperatures down to –47°C.

The main purpose of the studies was to get an idea of the range of oceanographic conditions in the area and to develop ideas about techniques, equipment and the required spacing of stations. Similarly, small programs in seismic sounding, gravity and geomagnetism provided useful information about subsurface conditions and materials.

The team started a physiographic study of Ellef Ringnes Island and established a glaciological party on the ice cap of Meighen Island. They also surveyed two more base lines: one across Amund Ringnes Island and the Fay Islands to Meighen Island and the other across Ellef Ringnes Island to Cape Isachsen and out over the Arctic Ocean. They now had the three base lines to fix the positions of the three stations that would form the basis of their navigational system.

The 1959 trip demonstrated the invaluable assistance of air support and the difficulties involved. The PCSP started the season with two aircraft, a Beaver and an Otter from McMurray Air Service Limited, Uranium City, Saskatchewan. Both aircraft were equipped with ski-wheels. They had to make as many as 12 landings a day, on floes or frozen leads in the sea ice. Each landing was in a new location on totally unprepared sur-

faces. Almost all of the flying was over the ocean at less than 150 m, often in poor visibility or white-out conditions. Navigational facilities were nonexistent; a magnetic compass is useless close to the magnetic pole and though there is continuous daylight in the summer, the sun may be hidden for weeks. To make matters worse, the emergency homing beacon at Isachsen broke down and could not be repaired until the autumn resupply airlift.

The Beaver soon showed that it could not withstand the severe buffeting of short take-offs and landings on the rough ice. On April 15, near the end of a landing run on an ice floe 100 km from shore, the Beaver's skiis were splayed apart and the undercarriage torn back. The Beaver ended up on its nose. The men were uninjured and were picked up the next day by the Otter. A few weeks later, after

Frank Hunt began as a topographical surveyor, had to learn all that logistical information about getting out there, then became an expert in logistics and stayed on as a manager, helping others to get out there. — Neil Anderson

Frank Hunt at the theodolite, on Prince Gustaf Adolf Sea in 1959. (photographer: Fred Roots)

emergency makeshift repairs, the Beaver was flown back to Isachsen by owner Bert Burry, who took off and landed on one temporary ski!

Over the next four months the weather deteriorated and the Otter was the Project's only aircraft. By the end of May the temperature had risen above freezing, and fog, low stratus clouds and snow flurries were common. By July the aircraft was landing in several inches of water on the melting sea ice. After that, the Otter had to land where the thawing permafrost was becoming sticky mud. Getting stuck in the mud was expected and required much shovelling by passengers and crew. Bert Burry and his engineer were already veterans of Arctic flying, but their performance under these most difficult conditions, without navigational support, and

isolated from spare parts, is still recalled with awe and respect.

Despite the difficulties, they did not lose their sense of humour. The sign on the aircraft service shack at Isachsen read:

McMurray Air Service Limited
deluxe Camping Trips in the Arctic,
Polar Bear rides our specialty.
Use no ticket — work your passage
— round trips no discount,
but may be discounted.
Our motto: Sic transit gloria semper
in gumbo (we may get stuck,
but with a good man on the shovel
we'll get there).

When Polar Shelf went north again in March of 1960, the program and the facilities were very different from those of the previous year. There were now two Otter aircraft, a twin-engine Beechcraft, one large and two small helicopters, six motor toboggans and a large tracked truck. Most important, they had a survey-navigational system. Using the information gained in the tests of 1959, the Decca Navigator Company in England had produced a survey system known as a 6f Lambda hyperbolic chain, or simply Decca. For the first time, every aircraft, field camp, survey station and fuel cache could be referred to by a set of inter-related coordinates. This system, now manned and maintained by a Canadian company, the Surnav Corporation, is still in operation.

There's the poor old Beaver with her legs knocked off. The whole fitting was broken, so we had to tie it on with rope. We took off with a one-legged Beaver. Yes, and we got home. — Fred Roots

There was a great spirit of adventure, and the Burrys were part of that — Bert Burry and his two sons Jim and George. They were there from the beginning, and they were there to make it happen. They pushed back the frontiers to get out there. — Neil Anderson

1959. (photographer: Fred Roots)

Don Smith, geophysicist, Adam Kerr, hydrographer and Frank Hunt, surveyor, are on traverse across a frozen Prince Gustaf Adolf Sea in 1959. A pressure ridge looms behind them. (photographer: Fred Roots)

Decca red camp on Borden Island in 1961. (photographer: Art Collin)

Erecting the Decca transmission mast at Isachsen in 1959. (photographer: Fred Roots)

The box contains dynamite to be used in seismic surveying south of Ellef Ringnes Island. (photographer: George Hobson)

"You have three stations: a master and two slaves, transmitting on different frequencies that are related to each other mathematically. At any point you can receive all three frequencies. The frequencies can be represented in lattices made up of interlacing parabolas. There is a master, a red and a green frequency. Master plus red will give you a position on the red lattice. Master plus green gives you a position on the green lattice. The point where they intersect is where you are."
— *George Hobson*

Isachsen now had its new radio beacon and portable ones were available for the outlying camps, in addition to the Decca system. A separate base camp was built alongside the weather station, which was linked to all aircraft and field camps with its own internal radio network. Equipment, personnel, spare parts and fresh food were delivered twice a month from southern Canada.

In 1960 the order of the day was full-scale, systematic survey and research of the continental shelf northwest of Meighen, Ellef Ringnes and Borden islands. By late April the Decca system was on the air and most activities were in full swing. At the peak of operations in early May,

Inuit neighbours at Grise Fiord in 1962. (photographer: Larry Sobczak)

Many years ago I began to feel that I was invading someone's backyard. I decided to do something about it. You have to realize that the Inuit have a different concept of their backyard — it stretches for hundreds of kilometres. I decided to start going into their settlements and talking to them, explaining what we were doing in their backyard. It took a long time, but gradually I became the contact. They aren't anti-science, but they want to be told what's going on. As a result, Polar Shelf has become a focal point for communications in the Arctic.
— George Hobson

Larry Sobczak, at left, does gravity work on Eglinton Island.
(photographer unknown)

70 scientists and technicians were in the field. Fifteen different surveys and investigations were carried out that summer, including hydrography, topographic surveys, oceanography, submarine geology, seismic survey, gravity, geomagnetism, geomorphology, glaciology, sea ice formations and distribution, engineering tests on the mechanical properties of sea ice, marine biology, botany, entomology and bacteriology.

Most units managed to carry out their programs successfully as planned. In addition, everyone involved continued to refine techniques and equipment to make future trips even more productive.

Back home, during the winter of 1960-1961, Polar Shelf tackled the problems of hydrography. It was the slowest and most labour-intensive of all the surveys and was demanding a disproportionate amount of personnel and logistical support.

"Hydrography was no different when Polar Shelf started than when Stefansson did his mapping back in 1913-14. You measured depths by drilling a hole through the ice and dropping a line down. If you hit bottom, you measured the depth. If you ran out of wire, you said 'no bottom.' The first year that we had an echo sounder to measure depth was 1961. In 1985, for the first time in the world, we had an airborne laser system in Simpson Strait to measure the depth of the water. We were able to take 90 000 measurements an hour."
— *Neil Anderson*

The staff developed light, compact echo-sounding equipment that could easily be carried on a small helicopter. The echo sounder would read the ocean depth through the ice — no need to drill 6 m holes. Hydrography could now keep up with and even force the pace of other survey work.

George Hobson on a traditional Inuit sled at Grise Fiord, 1960. (photographer: Mike Kelly)

Travel near Isachsen in 1960. (photographer: Denis St-Onge)

35

Hydrographer Ross Douglas at Resolute base in 1963.
(photographer: unknown)

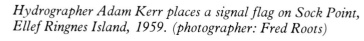

Hydrographer Adam Kerr places a signal flag on Sock Point, Ellef Ringnes Island, 1959. (photographer: Fred Roots)

Maclean Strait, Ellef Ringnes Island, 1981. (photographer: Michael Foster)

Hell Gate on Sverdrup Island in 1963. (photographer: R.M. Eaton)

Mike Eaton started off looking at the navigation system. We had errors in the data and we had to figure out what was causing them. There was no precedent, nothing to turn to. He developed methods of calibrating and evaluating navigation systems, which became his career. He is primarily responsible for pioneering the early hydrographic and navigation equipment up there.
— Neil Anderson

At the hydrographic camp on Prince of Wales Island in 1981, hydrographers and pilots plan the next day's soundings. (photographer: Michael Foster)

The Prince of Wales hydrographic camp in 1981, showing Parcolls. (photographer: Michael Foster)

Pierre Babusiaux was a character, very handsome, very worldly, real Parisian French. We think of those pilots as characters, but I suppose they're the products of the war. They're never home, their lives are risky and they live for the moment. Consequently you have people who are daring, open to risks, and always happy. It's true. If you are going to die tomorrow, why be sad, why pout about it?
— Neil Anderson

Pilot Pierre Babusiaux enjoys his morning Paris Match *at Hell Gate in 1963. (photographer: Ross Douglas)*

"Mayday! Mayday! JXR"

The dying JXR, 296 km north of Isachsen, 1961. Art Collin is climbing out of the aircraft. (photographer: Bernard Pelletier)

On April 29, 1961, Otter CF-JXR took off from Isachsen late in the evening on a routine submarine geology and oceanography mission. It was common practice to work the aircraft and some of the equipment round the clock during the long hours of light. The good weather was coming to an end and the pack ice was beginning to break up. Bert Burry was at the controls and his three passengers were Bernard Pelletier, geologist, Arthur Collin, oceanographer, and Horace Gardner, engineer and ice-drilling expert. They were headed for a position roughly 160 km off Meighen Island, about 320 km from Isachsen. Their exact position would not be known until they found a suitable landing place.

As he circled for a landing in the flat light of the midnight sun, Burry tried to radio his position to Isachsen. Base radio was busy. Rather than waste fuel on another circuit, Burry decided to land and report his position from the ground.

With the weight of the aircraft on the ice, the ski-wheels cut into the surface, throwing slush over the plane.

The ice was not old, solid sea ice as it appeared, but thin ice. The undercarriage broke through. As the Otter ploughed to a stop with its belly and struts in the water, Burry barely had time to send out a Mayday JXR call. Before he could give his position, the water rose around his knees and shorted out the radio. The others pulled themselves from the cabin and salvaged what emergency equipment they could reach. Most of the emergency gear was stowed behind heavy equipment and could not be removed.

Soon the four men were standing on safer ice at the edge of the floe, watching the Otter settle like a dead duck until its wings rested on the thin ice, its tail in the air and its nose in the sea. Only Collin and Gardner were dry. Pelletier was wet to the knees after trying to get equipment out of the cabin and Burry was soaked. They had not been able to reach the stove, tent, main box of food or radio. What they had was the aircraft engine blow-out heater, a small box of lunches, a tarpaulin, an axe and three sleeping bags of varying degrees of wetness. Collin climbed onto the Otter's wing, cut a hole in the top of the fuselage with the axe and retrieved Burry's sleeping bag, which was floating against the cabin roof. He also chopped off the luminescent glass fibre wingtips, which they used to support a makeshift tent.

As the others made camp, Burry kept himself warm by stamping out a message in the snow: OK NEED FUEL FOOD CLOTHING TENT. Then they all crawled into a snug little foxhole igloo lined with the tarpaulin and began to wait. To conserve food and fuel, they decided not to light the heater or break out rations until 24 hours had passed.

Their position was precarious. The temperature was about –40° C and the weather getting worse. The ice was about to break up and a good storm would delay any search until they had drifted well out of the area. They had limited supplies, they were wet, and had no assurance that their distress call had been heard. They would not be considered overdue for many more hours.

The Mayday call had been heard. By the time the party had made their camp, five PCSP aircraft were in the air. They were joined by two DC-3s,

which had been chartered by the Topographical Survey and happened to be at Isachsen delivering fuel. In the Arctic during an emergency, everyone helps.

The search was directed from Isachsen. Using the Decca equipment, searchers laid down a rigorous and complete search pattern. The aircraft swept back and forth along the Decca 'lanes.' The RCAF Search and Rescue authorities had been notified but before their aircraft could take off, a spotter on one of the DC-3s saw a mirror flash from Collin on the ice. A couple of hours later, a helicopter picked up the four men and took them back to Isachsen. They were in good condition. Only 29 hours had elapsed since they had left camp.

"When you're working with Polar Shelf, you're confident of the way the plane has been loaded, of the fuel and of the pilots. And then you've got the whole backup system. You've got radio contact — you know that if there's any problem they're going to come through for you. With Polar Shelf you have to check in twice a day, every day, so they can keep track of where you are and how you are."

— *David Gray*
Biologist, National
Museums of Canada

The 1961 season had its share of adventures, especially for Arthur Collin. On his next field trip he was camped on the sea ice to take oceanographic readings. Hearing a shuffling noise outside his tent, he grabbed his rifle and opened the tent flap. Not 5 metres away was a very large polar bear. The sound of the tent flap attracted the bear's attention and he rushed towards the opening. No time to aim — but no chance of missing such a colossal target.

Dr. Collin has a giant bearskin rug as a treasured memento of his years in the Arctic with the Polar Continental Shelf Project.

For seismologists Tony Overton and William Tyrlik, an encounter with a polar bear was a nightmare. They were camped near the edge of the Prince Gustaf Adolf Sea, west of Ellef

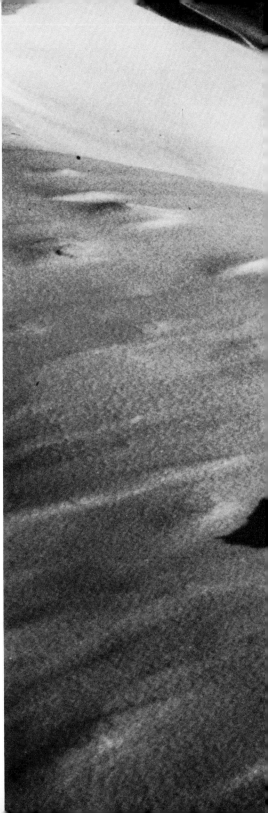

Ringnes Island. It was the end of May and the evening was so beautiful that they decided to sleep outside. Overton was awakened by being gently dragged across the snow in his sleeping bag. A bear had his forearm firmly, but tenderly, in its mouth. Overton's shouts awakened Tyrlik who grabbed the nearby rifle. Still encased in his sleeping bag, he tried to get off a clear shot at the bear without endangering Overton even further. Tyrlik's frantic contortions distracted the bear. It dropped Overton and charged at Tyrlik. The bear was shot as it lunged.

Tyrlik was unhurt. Overton had four small flesh wounds on his arm, and his sense of humour was still in excellent form:

"One of the luxuries of the Arctic is that you can participate in big-game hunting without bothering to get out of bed. It was the gentlest bear that ever dragged me."
— *Tony Overton*

Seismologist Tony Overton in 1960. (photographer: George Hobson)

A polar bear mother and cub on Somerset Island in 1984. (photographer: Al Koudys)

43

Coming of Age

For the first few years the Polar Continental Shelf Project operated out of Isachsen, first from the weather station and later from its own facilities. In 1964 the Project established its own base at Mould Bay on Prince Patrick Island. Four years later, as the Project shifted its area of study again, the Mould Bay camp was evacuated and a new base was established at Tuktoyaktuk. Today, the Polar Continental Shelf Project has two bases, at 'Tuk' and at Resolute. Each can accommodate about 50 people and provides facilities such as garages, stores and radio communications. In addition, there are small outposts at Alert, Devon Island, Bathurst Island and Mould Bay.

From the handful of scientists who conducted that first, tentative expedition in 1959, the project has grown into a major presence in the North.

Hydrographer Hans Pulkkinen is designing the Polar Shelf sign and crest to be hung at the base in Tuktoyaktuk. (photographer: Fred Alt)

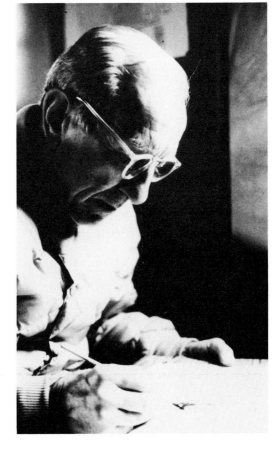

'Doc' George Sutton, often called the dean of American bird artists, works on Bathurst Island in 1969. (photographer: David Gray)

45

In 1985 there were 235 different scientific field parties in the Arctic Archipelago — more than 1000 people, all supported and sustained by PCSP.

"Over the last 25 years ... we might be looking at 20 000 to 25 000 people!"
— *George Hobson*

"If the wildlife of Canada, the native people of Canada and the scientists of Canada are making use of those so-called international waters, then that makes a stronger case for Canada's position.

"Through Polar Shelf, the islands have been inhabited a lot more than they would without Polar Shelf.... My time on Bathurst Island is certainly more extensive than even the oil company time there. A scientific research party has spent more time on that island than the oil companies, than the military, than the Inuit."
— *David Gray*

One of PCSP's cardinal rules is that no one is allowed to go out into the field alone. Consequently, a major fringe benefit of the Polar Continental Shelf Project has been the interaction of scientists from different disciplines. At any one time, the camps at Resolute and Tuktoyaktuk can be filled with geologists, geophysicists, biologists, oceanographers, archeologists, hydrographers, along with pilots, mechanics, engineers and radio technicians. Dining-hall conversation can cover an incredibly broad range of topics. This same interaction occurs daily, during the regular radio check-in of every field party. After everyone has been accounted for, the radio network is open so that parties can communicate with each other and report items that others might find useful or interesting.

This Bathurst Island lab building was erected for scientists from the National Museum of Natural Sciences in 1972. (photographer: David Gray)

David Gray watches muskox activities, 1969.
(photographer: Pierre Lamothe)

Geophysicist Jack Sweeney operates a gravity meter, 1973.
(photographer unknown)

Dorothy Van Eyk, botanist, at the site of an oil drill proposed for Polar Bear Pass on Bathurst Island in 1975. (photographer: David Gray)

Biologist David Gill bands an ivory gull on Seymour Island, 1971. (photographer: Stu MacDonald)

An ivory gull at Grise Fiord, 1970. (photographer: Stu MacDonald)

Botanist Sylvia Edlund working on Banks Island in 1974. (photographer: Jean-Serge Vincent)

"Another very appealing aspect for me is the fact that you meet other scientists . . . and you're able to exchange a lot of information. Other people note archeological sites and tell me. If I find a site on a certain beach ridge, this is of interest to the geologists and the geographers, because I can date the site and they can get information about the chronology of the various formations. Also, the biologists enhance my basic knowledge of the area by telling me about the bird life or the muskox population."

— Pat Sutherland
Archeologist, National
Museum of Man

"When I started working with plants in the Arctic I wanted to know why things grew where they did. Ellesmere Island seemed so much better than Cornwallis Island, but I didn't understand why. It wasn't until I realized that the difference was in the soils that I thought I've got to go with someone who understands the soils — a geologist."

— Sylvia Edlund
Botanist, Geological
Survey of Canada

"When I was working on ivory gulls on Seymour Island, we colour-marked and banded a lot of gulls. People in other camps knew of this program and periodically we would get reports from very distant camps saying that they had seen a colour-marked ivory gull and we could identify which bird it was and when we had marked it. So there was this continuous intermeshing and exchange which would be absolutely impossible without the connections Polar Shelf provided."

— Stu MacDonald
Biologist, National
Museums of Canada

"There's a lot of original work that's done under Polar Shelf's support. Many world authorities have passed through our doors."
— *George Hobson*

"We've seen great good come from, what shall I call it . . . the enforced intimacy of our passengers. When you get a botanist and a magnetician working together to load a drum of gas onto an airplane because they are both going to be working in the same area, they soon find out that they have more in common than a barrel of gas.

"It has been exciting to watch promising young scientists broaden their interests as a result of field work with scientists from other disciplines."
— *Fred Roots*

Except for the activities of the oil companies, the project coordinates the logistics for almost all the research in the Canadian Arctic. Support can take many forms: supplying aircraft, accommodation, fuel or communications. Some is provided free and some on the basis of partial or full cost

recovery, depending on the type of program, its importance to Arctic science and its resources.

Universities, government agencies and individuals all may apply to the Polar Continental Shelf Project for support of their research in the Arctic. Applications are screened by PCSP staff and by knowledgeable scientists in various disciplines from government agencies. For example, an application from a university for support of an archeological project will be evaluated by the Archeological Survey of Canada. Limited support is also extended to foreign universities.

"We have not been able for several years to support everybody who applies. I want to underline that we are interdepartmental in nature, so that other agencies can draw upon our resources, the same as our own department."
— *George Hobson*

"Right from the start, we opened our doors to any legitimate investigator who could contribute to PCSP's program and whose work seemed to fit in with our other studies."
— *Fred Roots*

The Polar Continental Shelf Project's flexibility has meant a great deal to students of the Arctic. In the past 25 years PCSP has supported more than 30 PhD applicants and many more masters students. Without PCSP, the high cost of Arctic research would have seriously hindered these men and women.

Though the possible presence of women on field parties concerned some agencies the Project had to work with, PCSP itself had no rules or regulations on the subject.

"If a person was qualified, we asked no questions about gender. All of our first experiences were so good, that our practice was never questioned. It became a non-issue very quickly."
— *Fred Roots*

"The first couple of days in the field, we would be watching each other very carefully, but after about a week, you sort of relax, you're one of the gang. I think that's the way it goes for most women who've worked up there."
— *Sylvia Edlund*

During most of its life, PCSP has been operating in an age of increasing governmental involvement in all facets of life. Polar Shelf saw its role differently. They wanted to remain small, innovative, able to respond quickly to changes in science and technology.

"The concept that the total operation of PCSP would be much greater than the sum of its parts proved itself right away. It has been one of the obvious strengths of PCSP ever since. But it took a while for its value in terms of integrated knowledge to be accepted. Twenty-five years ago, most persons concerned with scientific and technical fieldwork were associated with agencies that were strongly compartmentalized.

"There has been a lot of discussion about whether or not we made a mistake in not producing our own reports, in not building a scientific and technical organization — a polar research

A member of the Polar Shelf survey party in 1961 digs cooking snow from the Arctic Ocean 96 km north of the Sverdrup Islands. (photographer: Mike Eaton)

organization — to which people belonged. We'll never know whether we were right or not. Twenty-five years ago, I was firmly convinced that if we were going to produce hydrographic surveys acceptable to mariners around the world, the work should be done by someone from the Canadian Hydrographic Service, produced to Hydrographic Service standards, not just equivalent to them. I didn't think we should add to the scientific literature by starting up yet another series of in-house reports. Nor did I think we should isolate our scientists from the community in which they normally work. And, if the direction of science or technology should change, we could switch personnel and not be stuck with staff we no longer needed. I think that these decisions paid off scientifically and in effectiveness."
— *Fred Roots*

Archeology students Linda Jefferson and Dale Russell carefully sort artifacts at an excavation of a Dorset habitation site at Buchanan Lake in 1983. (photographer: Pat Sutherland)

Archeology got going in a big way in the High Arctic in the early 1970s, and that has a lot to do with Polar Shelf. It has to do with access. Without the logistical support they have provided free of charge, I simply couldn't raise the money to go. Logistics is a large chunk out of the budget of anyone who wants to work in that area. — Pat Sutherland

Sir William Parry's 1819 cabin, is photographed at Winter Harbour in 1981. (photographer: Doug McLeod)

Inside a Parcoll on the ice in Barrow Strait in 1983, marine biologists collect samples from the sea below. (photographer: Michael Foster)

Polar Shelf and Parks Canada decided to field a project to survey the Sir John Franklin sites before more people came in by helicopter and removed artifacts. Polar Shelf provided us with all of the logistics and food and equipment, and George Hobson was very much involved in the project. Our first week in the field, George was there, instructing on the use of the radio and how to get water when you don't have an immediate source, and this kind of thing. And he put the fear of God into me about being on time for plane pickups and making sure that I made the twice-daily weather scheds. After a time, Polar Shelf is like a family and you're glad to have that support network. I'm not sure I would go into that area without it. — Pat Sutherland

George Hobson at Beechey Island in 1976. (photographer unknown)

A lemming observes a biologist. The biologist is David Gill.
(photographer: David Gray)

> First you have your own shower, then with the same
> water you will do the laundry, then you will wash the
> floors. Water is costly — you have to chop the ice
> and melt it, and it takes a lot of work.
> — Hans Pulkkinen, hydrographer

1970. (photographer: Fred Alt)

Ellesmere Island in 1971. (photographer: Stu MacDonald)

Building the Body of Knowledge

After its first successful years the Polar Continental Shelf Project settled down to build a solid, accurate body of knowledge about the North. Often its official operating mandate was stretched to take advantage of opportunities. For example, the Decca was moved regularly to coincide with the study area, and from each position it could be used south of the mandate line, as well as north. It was an opportunity to gain more information at no additional cost. No one complained. Every bit of information that could be generated was useful and welcome.

Polar Shelf Goes to the Pole

In 1967 PCSP and the Dominion Observatory went to the North Pole. The main objectives of this geophysical expedition were to establish a line of gravity stations from Alert to the North Pole and to obtain as many gravity observations as possible near the Pole, across the Lomonosov Ridge (an undersea mountain range). In addition, they wished to develop and test new techniques for precise navigation in the polar region.

"We had a base camp at Alert and I had helicopters. So we planned on putting temporary gas caches on the ice between Alert and the Pole. There would be camps, temporary airstrips and back-up Otters all along the way. It was to be a totally safe, backed-up operation.

"What happened was that the fog socked the Otters in at Isachsen, the ice was beginning to break up and we were running out of time. After many hours of going through all the options, we took a very old aircraft, the Bristol Freighter, with no gas caches along the way, no back-up and no checked-out airstrips. Seven of us got in that old bucket of bolts and headed for the Pole. It would be hard to say if we'd do it today or not.

"When we got up there we had to find an area flat enough and smooth enough for a landing. The ice had to be old and thick enough to support the aircraft.

The 1967 North Pole expedition, manned by Neil Anderson, hydrographer; Hans Weber, geophysicist; Axel Geiger, of the Geodetic Survey of Canada; Robert Lillestrand, a space navigation specialist; Mike Pearlman, of the Ocean Research Corporation; Robert Iverson, of the U.S. Army Map Service; and Leif Lundgaard, technician. (photographer: Hans Weber)

Neil Anderson at the Pole, 1967. (photographer unknown)

At 30 below, that's fine, you can work. During storms
I develop a very great appetite — I eat all the time.
— Hans Pulkkinen

1967. (photographer: Hans Pulkkinen)

First PCSP landing at the North Pole in 1967. The ice is being drilled to find out if it is thick enough to hold the aircraft. (photographer: Hans Weber)

Hans Weber at the Pole in 1967. (photographer: Neil Anderson)

"The procedure was that you come down and thump the ice and you take off and come around to see if there are any wet spots. Don Braun, a very experienced older fellow, was the pilot. His copilot was a rooky straight out of the airforce who was used to flying jets.

"This old aircraft sounded as if it was collapsing every time we hit. When we landed, before we shut the engines off, we had to leap out and measure the depth of the ice. That was my job. So with the engines going full blast, ready to take off, I jumped out onto the ice with a one-inch auger and cranked it through."

— *Neil Anderson*

Gravity experiments, which showed that a plumb line — a line with a weight at the end — suspended over the Pole did not hang straight but deflected some 30 degrees to the east, indicated that the Lomonosov Ridge had a mass deficiency, that is, there was some material of a lower density imbedded in the crust. This information, which suggested that the ridge is a fragment from Siberia's Barents Shelf, led to the later LOREX studies in 1979.

The group stayed at the Pole from May 6 to May 14. Even though many of the experiments planned for the expedition had to be curtailed, the knowledge gained about navigation in the polar area proved to be invaluable for planning the next trip. The old Bristol Freighter was retired and mounted on a pillar near Yellowknife airport.

Getting Back to Basics During 1967 and 1968 many of the scientists who had been attached to the Project returned to their original departments. This was so they could obtain more professional interaction with their colleagues and also to prevent PCSP from becoming institutionalized. As other departments and agencies began to use the Project, the scientists attached to PCSP found themselves exercising their logistical experience more than their profession. A small group stayed with PCSP.

"The first two years I was there, I was able to do seismic surveys, but I am no longer a geophysicist doing seismology. There's no way I have time to

The old Bristol Freighter, this old bucket of bolts is what we took, with no gas caches along the way, no back-ups, and no checked-out airstrips. Seven of us got in that airplane and headed for the Pole.
— Neil Anderson

1967. (photographer: Neil Anderson)

A tense return from the second North Pole expedition, 1969, via Twin Otter, with Axel Geiger; Leif Lundgaard; Frank Adams, the technician in charge of the Omega positioning equipment; Mike Pearlman; and in the background, the Omega. (photographer: Hans Weber)

pursue a project — the administration is just too much. But there's so much going on — that's why it's so exciting.

"There are some 2700 items in our bibliography, and I've at least read the abstract on every one of them. I wouldn't swap my job for anybody's. Here you've got the whole gamut of science in an area that's just so darned interesting."

— *George Hobson*

Back to the Pole In 1969 an expedition returned to the Pole. They landed on April 2 and stayed until May 3, to take advantage of the clear weather and the visibility of the stars because of the sun's low angle.

The expedition carried a Magnavox transit satellite receiver. Its raw data were recorded on punched paper tape and processed in Ottawa after the expedition returned. The Twin Otter aircraft used for spot gravity measurements and depth soundings had an experimental Omega receiver on board to receive a very low frequency signal used for navigation.

Despite a four-day storm, which blew the ice station 40 km to the southeast, the expedition was a success.

A New Concern: the Environment In the early 1970s PCSP's methods of working in the North were changing. New land-use regulations required much more care of the environment.

Pilot Harvey Easton, 1969. (photographer unknown)

Harvey Easton flew a lot for the hydrographic people. We did a lot of flying — in my first two years, it was over 200 hours a month. The helicopter was integral to the survey operation. Harvey was a hard-drinking, gambling, tough guy. He had no eyebrows and big knuckles, and that was from fights. When Harvey won at gambling, he usually bought beer and dropped it off to the hydrographers. A real character, and a good pilot. — Neil Anderson

"In the early days, you put out a bunch of drums and you left them. We've had to spend a lot of money and a lot of time to clean up old food caches and drum caches. Now it's just part of our philosophy. If you put a drum in, a drum has to come out. It's only common sense, and now we find that we can clean up without having to make extra trips. The land-use regulations were needed — otherwise the place was going to be a dump, from one end to the other. It's a pity we didn't have them from the start."
— *George Hobson*

A Change in Command — but the Work Goes On In 1972 Fred Roots accepted a position in headquarters of the Department of Energy, Mines and Resources and later went to the Department of the Environment as senior science advisor.

George Hobson was named as the new director of the Polar Continental Shelf Project. As the chief of the Seismic Section, Geophysics Division, Geological Survey of Canada, he had been involved in PCSP activities since 1960 and was no stranger to either the people or the philosophy of the Project.

One helicopter changes the transmission on another after a crash landing in 1969. (photographer: Hans Pulkkinen)

Divers in air-insulated dry suits work at the AIDJEX project in 1972. (photographer: Hans Weber)

There were many projects that had to be continued, such as the sea-ice atlas and the Arctic Ice Dynamics Joint Experiment.

From 1960 PCSP pilots and many others had kept records of sea-ice conditions in the Arctic Archipelago, since regular ice patrols in the Arctic did not go into those areas. The results of 19 years of observations were published in 1975, 1977 and 1981 in the three-volume *Sea-Ice Atlas of Arctic Canada*, which was eagerly snapped up by oil companies and others interested in northern navigation.

AIDJEX — The Arctic Ice Dynamics Joint Experiment AIDJEX had been started in 1970 to study the large-scale interaction between the hydrosphere and the atmosphere in the Arctic Ocean. This was a multidisciplinary, multiagency, multinational project supported by the U.S. National Science Foundation and the Polar Continental Shelf Project. Scientists from Canada, the United States and Japan were involved.

Five years of field and laboratory experiments were needed to develop the special observation equipment needed for AIDJEX and to refine the mathematical theory involved in its objectives.

We were flying at about 500 feet, and suddenly the helicopter just dipped, just like that, and nobody knew what was going on. And there was no communication. The pilot started to look for a place to land because he wanted to go down fast, but the ice was so ragged there. Finally he landed. I stepped out and looked and I saw that the big huge rotor was just hanging. I said to the pilot, 'Wally, come out, you're only hanging on by half an inch.' He said, 'Oh, come on.' Then he got out and looked and said, 'Oh my God!' The rotor was completely out and lying loose on one end. Just one more second and it would have gone. And we were on ice and there was a very strong current and we were 20 km from shore. That was a close one. — Hans Pulkkinen

From March 1975 to May 1976, four manned stations, equipped with special observation buoys, drifted in the Beaufort Sea. The buoys measured atmospheric motion, wind stress, ice strain, water motion and water stress, and transmitted the data via satellite to recording stations on shore. In addition, continuous depth and gravity measurements and a seismic refraction survey were carried out by the Earth Physics Branch. This was the largest scientific operation ever undertaken in the Arctic Ocean. It yielded basic information that ultimately affected the design of offshore drilling rigs, drilling ships and artificial islands.

Bun and Bloodface The physical sciences occupied a great deal of time and attention but the other sciences were not neglected. Botanists, biologists, archeologists and zoologists have all been helped by PCSP.

"I travelled for several years by myself, as far as 60 km from a weather station. I would be gone for a week and I carried everything on my back. The specimens you can collect are limited to what you can carry on foot.

"Now [since Polar Shelf] you can be dropped off in a remote area either by Twin Otter or helicopter and if you've got something you can't carry, the helicopter will move it for you. Flying up through rock valleys in a helicopter, I've picked up new records of birds' range extensions. There was no way that I would have been able to cover all that area on foot. So another plus for Polar Shelf is that it increases your efficiency so much, and adds a great deal more depth to your research."

— *Stu MacDonald*

The depth of research that PCSP makes possible has resulted in some fascinating experiences and unique learning opportunities for scientists.

"In the fall of '73, there were two arctic hares in the vicinity of the station on Bathurst. When we came back in April '74, one hare was still there. We moved into his territory and he didn't move out. As biologists, we initiated contact with him and named him 'Bun.' We offered him fresh carrots . . . then we got more daring and offered him a handful of rolled oats, which he eventually would take from our hands and we could tickle him under the chin. It was very useful, biologically; it meant we could get closeup photographs. It's very frustrating that you're always looking at your animals through a telescope, and that you can't see the colour of their eyes and how their nose works. But with this guy, you could be right there and that was a wonderful experience. We even enticed him onto a toboggan and pulled him around . . . so there were some unique behavioural experiences on both sides."

— *David Gray*

"We didn't see very many animals in the midwinter period. And there were very few sounds in our environment. Once you got out of camp, the only noise you heard was the wind blowing around your parka . . . sometimes the sound of the snow if you were walking . . . and sometimes the Ski-Doo, if you happened to get it started. The only other sound we had for the whole three months was the sound of the wolves howling.

"Every so often you'd wake up in the middle of the night to the sound of the wolves howling, just a few metres away, on the edge of the camp. That was the neatest feeling of the whole winter, to know that there were wolves out there somewhere. They would visit the camp when we were away. In

1970-71. (photographer: David Gray)

70

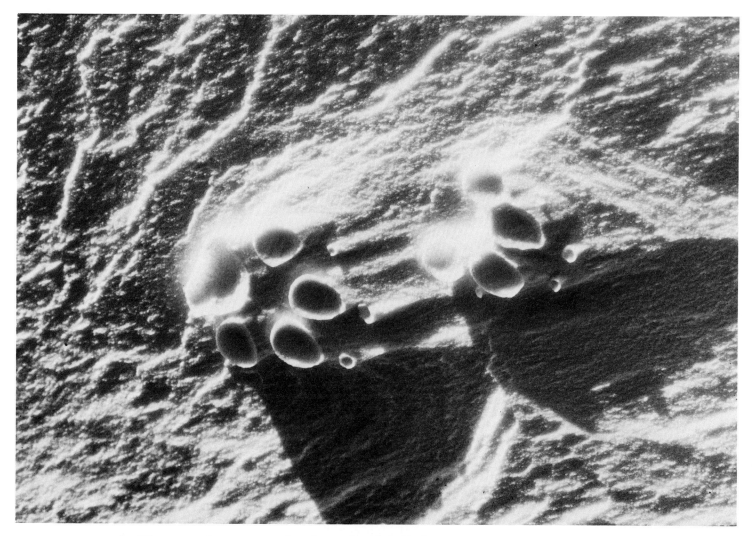

These tracks were made after a fresh fall of snow, so the weight of the wolf pressed the snow down, and then the wind came and blew the snow away. But where the pressure was just right, the track remained. The little cups of the pads were on pedestals. They had the feeling of fine china.
— David Gray

March, we went to see the muskox carcass they had killed and they would visit our camp, while we were visiting theirs.

"I first saw Bloodface running towards a muskox from a hundred metres away. He proceeded to attack and kill the muskox, but the battle lasted for an hour. After feeding on the carcass, he left it. Since I was overdue back at camp, Phillip Taylor, an ornithologist who was with us at that time at camp, had come out on the Ski-Doo to meet me. I was walking back toward camp. The wolf had left the carcass, then come back to it, picking up my tracks, and began following me. So Phillip was coming up one way and the wolf the other way, and I was in the middle. As soon as Phillip came, we shut off the machine and Bloodface walked right up to us. He had blood all over his face and down under his neck. It was my impression that he had never seen humans before. I shot off a whole roll of film and while I was reloading, Phillip started to play with the wolf by jumping around and the wolf responded by jumping back and forth a bit. Eventually he left us and followed the Ski-Doo track back towards camp."

— *David Gray*

Bun, the noted Arctic hare, 1974. (photographer: David Gray)

"We went back to get the muskox carcass and Bloodface followed us. The carcass was too big for the toboggan and Bloodface followed along, trying to get the carcass back. After we dragged the carcass back to camp he adopted us. He used to sleep within sight of camp on a nearby ridge. We gave the carcass to him eventually and we know he used it for two years."
— *Stu MacDonald*

"He was by himself that year, but the following year he came back with a female, who became known as the Ghost. When we first saw him that season, he had a streak of blood on his face again."
— *David Gray*

LOREX and CESAR In the spring of 1979 Energy, Mines and Resources Canada mounted a full-scale, multi-disciplinary project called LOREX to study the nature and origins of the Lomonosov Ridge. The ridge is an underwater mountain range 3000 m high, which runs from the continental shelf off Greenland and Ellesmere Island to the Siberian continental shelf. It had been discovered by the Russians in 1949 and first revealed in

A crack severs the LOREX camp. The cold Arctic Ocean is below the bridge, 1979. (photographer: Hans Weber)

Base manager Fred Alt checks the latest crack in the airstrip during LOREX, 1979. (photographer: Roger Belanger)

A Hercules aircraft is unloaded at Project CESAR, 1983.
(photographer: Hans Weber)

Hans Weber emerges from under the ice during LOREX, 1979. (photographer unknown)

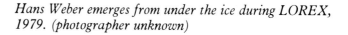

To us, working with Polar Shelf, the most significant thing has been individuals — guys like Eddy Chapman, Frank Hunt, Fred Alt, George Hobson and Fred Roots. And not just those people but the mechanics, and the guys who come over and help unload the aircraft, and teach you how to build a Parcoll. Right from day one, virtually everyone we've encountered from Polar Shelf has been a nice guy. — David Gray

Fred Alt radios the PCSP base in Resolute Bay, during the LOREX project in 1979. (photographer: Roger Belanger)

Valery Lee does experiments in physical oceanography during EUBEX (Eurasian Basin Experiment) off Greenland in 1981. (photographer: Peter Jones)

a map published in 1954. That map had caused a sensation among Arctic experts outside the Soviet Union, who had been unaware of the scope and scale of Soviet exploration in the Arctic.

The LOREX program was planned and coordinated by the Earth Physics Branch of EMR with logistical support provided by PCSP. Scientists from other branches of EMR, from the Department of Fisheries and Oceans, and from universities in Canada and the United States took part.

A main camp and two satellite camps 60 km from the main camp were established on drifting sea ice near the North Pole on March 21, 1979. As the camps drifted across the ridge, their positions were continuously tracked and computed by satellite and on-line satellite receiver. The accuracy of these navigational fixes was within 250 m. Based on hundreds of echo and shallow seismic soundings, the scientists were able to prepare a highly detailed 100 m contour map of the seafloor area around the North Pole.

The Lomonosov Ridge has steep sides and a flat top between 25 km and 200 km wide, which seems to indicate that it was formed by shifting land masses, not volcanic action. The geological information from borehole samples and from mapping provided valuable insights into the formation of the Canadian continental shelf margin.

Under the ice of the Arctic Ocean are three parallel mountain ranges; the Lomonosov Ridge is the middle one. The Nansen-Gakkel Ridge is on the Eurasian side and the Alpha Ridge on the Canadian side. The Alpha Ridge was discovered in 1963.

The Alpha Ridge extends 1300 km from Ellesmere Island, halfway across the Arctic Ocean, to just west of the North Pole. It is between 250 km and 400 km wide and almost 3 km high and it poses some interesting questions. If it is a fragment of the Siberian continent that shifted eastward it may have oil-bearing sediments. If it was created by the spreading of the seafloor, it may have minerals usually associated with volcanic eruptions. If the Alpha Ridge is definitely attached to the Canadian polar continental shelf off Ellesmere Island, then it will represent a natural extension of Canadian territory.

Planning for the Canadian Expedition to Study the Alpha Ridge (CESAR) was begun while LOREX was also being planned. The logistics for CESAR were enormous and called for all of PCSP's experience and expertise, because the equipment requirements were gigantic.

Hans Weber was the chief scientist on both LOREX and CESAR. He flew across the Alpha Ridge in February 1983 and, with the aid of side-looking radar, found suitable sites to build two runways. By early March, the Department of National Defence was delivering 300 000 kg of equipment and supplies in Hercules aircaft, making up to six flights per day. Research began on March 25 and continued for the next 60 days.

The heavy equipment was necessary to get piston core samples and gravity cores from the ridge and its flanking basins. The cores produced by CESAR were an average of 4.7 m long and some were over 5.5 m — much longer than any others ever removed from the Arctic. The information carried in these cores is helping to delineate the history of the Arctic Ocean through its geological evolution and climatic history.

There is a three-million-year history of the Arctic Ocean in most of the CESAR cores. One core actually contains a perfectly preserved record of plankton from the warm sea of the Cretaceous Era.

Scientists at EMR's Atlantic Geoscience Centre and at Dalhousie University and the University of Toronto are working on those cores. At the time of writing, their conclusions are eagerly awaited.

"There was a period in the late '70s when we were putting out 'bush fires.' Now we are getting down to doing regular and regulated science."
— *George Hobson*

What was really important to Leif was skiing. It was through Leif and the plastic ski bindings he lent me for our winter work that we really learned how to walk in the Arctic. Introducing cross-country skis to my work in the winter was a major stride forward.
— *David Gray*

Leif Lundgaard on the LOREX project in 1979. (photographer: Hans Weber)

I've seen Leif working out in very cold weather and he seems almost oblivious to the discomfort and just goes right on with what he is doing. I can't imagine Polar Shelf being as effective if they lose this personal relationship with many of the individuals, the ones who go back year after year on continuing projects. Because Polar Shelf is so helpful, we have a responsibility not to disappoint them.
— *Stu MacDonald*

Leif Lundgaard on Penny Ice Cap in 1966. (photographer: Hans Weber)

If they're respected scientists and you think they're going to get something, you send someone like Leif with them, just to take care of them.
— George Hobson

Technician Leif Lundgaard works on the ice drill at Mer de Glace Agassiz Ice Cap in 1977. (photographer: Peter Reshitnyk)

**Leif can even stand up and growl off a polar bear. At Mould Bay, when they were retrieving old oil drums from the beach, they were surprised by a bear hunkered down behind the drums. It stood up on its hind legs and growled at Leif, so Leif made himself as big as possible and growled back. It upset the bear just enough to give Leif time to get away.
— David Gray**

Sun dogs over Axel Heiberg Island. (photographer: Peter Reshitnyk)

Surveying with a distomat, Mer de Glace Agassiz Ice Cap, 1979. (photographer: Peter MacKinnon)

A Thule habitation site on Bathurst Island, photographed in 1974. (photographer: David Gray)

Leif Lundgaard descends an ice hole for glaciology studies at Mer de Glace Agassiz Ice Cap in 1977. (photographer: Peter Reshitnyk)

Some of the most beautiful times in the Arctic are in the fall and late fall, when you get the low sun, beautiful cloud effects and sun on the snow. You have sunsets that last several hours.

Sometimes the whole countryside can be steeped in the gorgeous rose colour. You get all shades of reds and pinks and purples — all except pure white.

In late February, March and early April, you can have days that are nothing but pink and blue. Everything the sun touches is pink, and everything in shadow is blue. — David Gray and Stu MacDonald

Lenticular clouds over Melville Island in 1977. (photographer: Dave Pugh)

Silt sediments at the end of a gully, Banks Island, 1977.
(photographer: Jean-Serge Vincent)

Braya purpurescens, *purplish braya, Melville Island.* *(photographer: Sylvia Edlund)*

We used to think that whatever landed there and could survive, grew. There was just no sense to it. The reality is almost the opposite of that. The vegetation is so tightly controlled by the materials. But the materials are all dirty-grey looking, and unless you're working with geologists you don't notice the differences. When I realized that the difference was materials, I thought, hey, I've got to go with somebody who understands materials. *— Sylvia Edlund*

Vaccinium vitis-idaea, *mountain cranberry, northern Keewatin, 1976. (photographer: Sylvia Edlund)*

This 4000-year-old harpoon head was found on Devon Island. (photographer: Robert McGhee)

I've seen that many times. It isn't often that you will find that red colour — the sun has to be right, coming from the west. There are three Franklin graves there, and one from Belcher's time. That's Erebus and Terror Bay. And Captain Doug McLeod (pilot with Bradley Air Services), Captain Ho-Ho, we called him. Because he's always laughing, ho-ho, ho-ho. It's just his mannerism. His heart is as big as his body. — George Hobson

Hydrographer Adam Kerr stands on the cairn where a message from Bernier, the early Arctic explorer, was found in 1961. (photographer: Neil Anderson)

Erebus and Terror Bay. (photographer: Doug McLeod)

Subsea photography, Dundas polynya, 1980. (photographer: Brian Smiley)

Biologist Stu MacDonald makes up bird specimen skins on Bathurst Island, 1968. (photographer: David Gray)

Rime-covered transmission towers on Ellesmere Island, 1966.
(photographer: Neil Anderson)

Project CESAR, the Canadian Expedition to Study the Alpha Ridge, 1983. (photographer: Peter Bregg, Canapress)

Around the camps, there's always somebody wanting to go somewhere, or wanting to know why he can't go somewhere, or wanting to know where he can get this or that. And you're just a mother to the flock of chicks. — George Hobson

Mer de Glace Agassiz Ice Cap, 1976.
(photographer: Peter MacKinnon)

Blowing snow and clouds over Bathurst Island in 1977.
(photographer: David Gray)

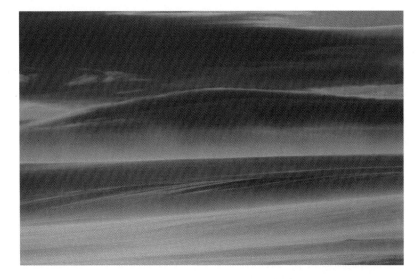

It can be beautiful at times, and I think one of the things that struck me is that it's one part of the world where you can be in absolute stillness. You don't realize how much of the world is noise until you get somewhere where the silence is really deafening. When we were in Jones Sound in 1982 . . . the beautiful sunny days, just beautiful days, twenty-four hours a day, no wind, comfortable temperatures. Then the fog rolled in and we never saw a thing the rest of the time. — Brian MacLean, geologist

Bull muskox at Sverdrup Pass. (photographers: David Gray and Rick Popko)

Northern Lougheed Island. (photographer: Sylvia Edlund)

Archer Fiord, Ellesmere Island — "a magical country."
(photographer: Pat Sutherland)

We were helicopter-surveying for early paleo-Eskimo sites in 1983. That was a very exciting day, because we found quite a number of sites, among them a site of the Independence II culture, which is a relatively rare thing . . . there are only four more known sites. That day the pilot was Jerry Dionne. He was very interested in Arctic archeology, and he helped look for sites . . . it was a magical day, and a magical country. — Pat Sutherland

Admiralty Inlet, Cape Crauford, 1984.
(photographer: Rick Riewe)

95

Bloodface, the wolf who visited the camp on Bathurst Island in 1969. (photographer: David Gray)

Glaciologist Roy 'Fritz' Koerner on traverse during his studies. (photographer: Peter Reshitnyk)

Leffert Glacier, Ellesmere Island. (photographer: Peter MacKinnon)

The gullies are unexpectedly dangerous . . . you must be very careful when you are riding a motor toboggan. A big, huge toboggan goes all over the place. That's how it is. The ground has little snow on it, so you pick a nice little gully where there is snow . . . and the next thing you know, right in the middle of the gully a crack appears and then there is a ravine with a sloping shoulder of snow and this Ski-Doo is slicing downhill with half a ton of gear on it. That was pretty tricky. — Gus Vilks, geologist

A plane is pulled to break out its frozen skis. (photographer: Peter Reshitnyk)

Roy Koerner monitors ice core equipment used for glaciology studies, Mer de Glace Agassiz Ice Cap, 1979. (photographer: Peter Reshitnyk)

Using an ice drill, on Devon Ice Cap in 1973. (photographer: Peter MacKinnon)

> **An awful lot of people in the field have their evening meal at the same time as the weather 'sched'. You're on the family line, you know what's going on. We call the camps by name, so that people know where others are, and they know what the weather is like in various places. Then they can do some of their own planning. — George Hobson**

Technician Charlie Roots and glaciologist Peter MacKinnon at camp on Devon Island Ice Cap, 1977. (photographer: Peter Reshitnyk)

Glaciology base camp on Devon Island in 1973. Ski-Doos and Nansen sleighs are two of the best means of ground travel. (photographer: Peter Reshitnyk)

Mealtime at Resolute in 1985. This is one of the most important times of the day, where everyone meets and exchanges information. This table includes Barry Hough, base manager, Peter Osborne, technician, and GSC technician Robbie Burns. (photographs from p.100 to 127 by Michael Foster, except where noted otherwise)

Barry Hough and George Hobson at Resolute in 1985. George has spent the morning on the telephone getting back in touch after spending many weeks on the ice island.

Resolute is a unique working base, in that you can taxi your airplane off the airstrip and you are at your place of business. You can get within a hundred yards of your front door and park your airplane. Within the last few years, if Polar Shelf hadn't been there, there would have been a heck of a lot less activity. There's hardly ever a time when we go into Resolute and we land, that I don't say, 'Home again!'
— George Hobson

Susan Baker, cook at Resolute in 1985, and George Hobson.

At Resolute in 1985. Barry Hough, base manager, is on the radio for the twice-daily schedule.

George Benoit, technician, and Lausanne Losier, hydrographer, unload supplies at Resolute in 1985.

Polar Continental Shelf Project base, Resolute Bay, May 1985.

PART II   ISLAND IN THE ICE

"I wouldn't swap my job for anybody's." — *George Hobson*

Although much of the Arctic is frozen, rocky and barren, very little stands still. There is always change and motion. There, more than anywhere else, one can feel the floating nature of the earth's crust. The following account by Fred Roots describes how an entire 'island' was found to have traveled from the west coast of Ellesmere Island to a point 1400 km away in the middle of the Beaufort Sea, and of how scientists came to see such a moveable ice island as an ideally cost-efficient, moveable scientific base.

"In 1959, while running a survey around the northwest end of Ellef Ringnes Island, we came across a low range of rocky hills at about 79°25′N 106°W. There was no previous record of rocky hills in the area — the north end of Ellef Ringnes Island is low, with sand and frozen mud, and so flat that it is very hard to tell where the shoreline is in winter. When we investigated, we found that the rocks were all igneous granitic and dioritic — quite different from anything on the nearby islands for hundreds of kilometres. If there really were granitelike intrusions in this part of the Sverdrup Basin, the prospects for oil would be dim, for it would mean that the rocks had been subjected to temperatures and pressures incompatible with the retention of petroleum.

"So I busied myself with geology, Frank Hunt set up his survey stations, and Larry Sobczak set up his gravity meter on some big stable rocks. Suddenly we heard Larry shout, 'We're moving!' Sure enough, his very sensitive gravity meter showed that the whole range of hills was slowly heaving and settling, just as a coastal plain does, inland from heavy surf. But there was no surf for thousands of miles. We were not on a hilly island, but probably on a fantastically large pile of debris on top of floating ice, likely grounded in the shallow water off Cape Isachsen, but still heaved by tide and waves. I took photos and rock samples.

"Eventually, we matched the rock samples and found that the debris probably came from a glacier near Phillips Inlet, on the west coast of Ellesmere Island.

"A year or so later an oil geologist friend of mine was in the Arctic and Antarctic Institute in Leningrad and saw there a map, marked with an island off Cape Isachsen. He contacted me, and I could reassure him that we knew about it, but that it was not a real island but an enormous ice floe or piece of glacier ice with the

An old communications hut left on ice island T3. By 1962 erosion has left it on a pedestal. (photographer: George Hobson)

A DC-3 lands on skis on the ice island. The runway is not yet built.

damnedest pile of stones on it you ever did see. And it was gone again.

"In the winter of 1961-62, the front cover of a booklet from the U.S. Office of Naval Research showed a familiar scene: the rocky debris hills that I had studied so carefully. Scientists from the ONR Arctic Research Laboratory at Point Barrow had discovered it in the middle of the Beaufort Sea, and had placed a research station on it, dubbing it ARLIS II, Arctic Research Laboratory Ice Station II. That spring, pilot Bert Burry and I arranged to visit ARLIS II. As soon as we landed, we were sure. There was the large rock where Larry had set his gravity meter; there was the debris from my rock sampling, now 1400 km from where I had first smashed the rocks. In three years, nothing else had changed except that some snow had melted.

"I picked up some hammered fragments, took them back to Ottawa, and found that one was the exact mate to a piece I had brought back three years before. It must be very seldom that a geologist gets to sample the same natural rock twice in two different locations. The incident was a dramatic demonstration of Arctic oceanographic and geological processes, and showed the value of coordinated and continuing science programs."
— *Fred Roots*

ARLIS II was not quite a 'real island' — it was an ice island, a large, floating chunk of freshwater ice — and it was Polar Shelf's first contact with the phenomenon. Ice islands only come into being, or calve, in any decent size about every 20 years, and only from the north end of Ellesmere Island, either from the front of the Ward Hunt Ice Shelf or from three fiords — Disraeli, Yelverton or Milne. They come from ice shelves formed by the runoff of fresh water from the land. The shelf grows and moves out from land and after a time there is enough buoyancy that a large piece breaks off and floats away.

Around 1960 five pieces were calved. Before that, in 1940 or 1941, three pieces were calved, but not discovered until 1946, when they were dubbed T1, T2 and T3. T3 was occupied and studied for brief periods until the late 1950s, primarily by scientists from the United States. Our ice island, 'the biggest piece of property we have right now,' as George Hobson puts it, was probably calved in late 1982 from the Ward Hunt Ice Shelf. There were five pieces in this calving that were big enough for an airplane to land on. The ice is very old, between 2700 and 4000 years old, and very pure. A core sample taken from the ice shelf showed no seawater throughout the 45 m length of the core — all was freshwater ice.

If you were to fly over a vast, ice-clogged area, you could spot an ice island immediately from its corrugations, looking soft and rounded from the air: the 'range of hills' described by Fred Roots. At one time, it was a flat surface. One theory for the formation of these hills and troughs is that long, travelling melt puddles developed. Little puddles develop in the summertime (a little dust draws the sunlight), the prevailing wind blows over them from one end and water piles up at the other. The deeper end becomes a darker blue, which draws more sunlight, and the puddles melt faster and begin to move in the direction of more melt. Before long, the puddle stretches out and becomes a trough, so the ice island becomes characterized by corrugations about 100 m from peak to peak and 2 m or 3 m deep in the trough.

The Ward Hunt Ice Shelf off northern Ellesmere Island in 1971 shows the corrugations that will characterize the ice islands that calve from it. (photographer: Stu MacDonald)

Tom Krochak, ice island cook from 1984 to 1986.

Another characteristic of ice islands is that they tend to float off into the 'Arctic gyre' (clockwise rotation of water in the Arctic Ocean). Depending on winds and currents, they will break off along the northwest coast of Ellesmere Island, float down along the coasts of the Queen Elizabeth Islands, into the Beaufort Sea, along the Alaskan coast, perhaps along the Russian coast, up around the Pole and down along the coast of Greenland, taking about 20 years to do the circuit. Some will describe a smaller circle, and spend 40 years going round and round the Arctic Ocean. Some will stall at midpoint, some will get blown into one of the sounds or passages among the islands and get stuck, some will blow back against an island coast and ground themselves. George Hobson would like our ice island . . .

"to come down the northwest coast, across the Beaufort Sea. Off the tip of Alaska, about Barrow, we'd like it to head in a northerly direction, not to go too far over onto the Soviet coast. It's like being on the end of a piece of string when you get on that gyre. If it's a long string, you can end up going across the Lomonosov Ridge, in which case your ice island is lost; it goes out the east side of Greenland. If

He's a good cook. One day he stood up there and said, 'I have an announcement to make. As long as we have 34 people in camp, one of you is going to wash the dishes and one of you is going to dry the dishes at lunch and at dinner. And if you don't want to do that, then you're not going to eat.' And he made it stick. He's the type of fellow you wanted to help. — George Hobson

you're on a short string, it's going to stay in the gyre and make three, maybe four, excursions around the Arctic Ocean. If we could have it make even a second pass, we'd have the use of it for 15 to 20 years."

Why does anyone want to be on a chunk of ice in the middle of the Arctic Ocean for 20 years? Partly to find out when the Arctic Ocean opened up to become an ocean. North America and Europe were once joined together and there was no Atlantic Ocean. The Arctic Islands also were probably part of the continent, joined to Canada or Alaska or Russia, and the Arctic Ocean wasn't there. Sections of the earth's surface tend to rise, fall and move around. If we are to claim it as our own, we have to determine just what comprises our continental shelf. We need to know our geological roots.

"As the years go by, as we move along the North American Plate on the ice island, as it moves down the west coast of the Queen Elizabeth Islands towards the Beaufort Sea, along the Alaskan shelf and the Soviet shelf, and stays in the Arctic Ocean Basin, we'll be able to tell more about the geology of the basin. We'll know more about how the Siberian Plate and the North American Plate have interacted, about how North America and Alaska have

been contiguous. We can find the date of the Arctic Ocean, its structure, the structure of the Lomonosov Ridge, the Alpha Ridge, the Nansen Ridge. We'll know more about the general history of the whole north of the world."

— *George Hobson*

If the ice island does as scientists hope, it could become a traveling base of study for the whole Arctic Ocean basin, the year round. The LOREX and CESAR camps were on pack ice. They could be inhabited only after the sun returned in the spring, and had to

be abandoned before the ice broke up in summer, giving scientists only two months in which to work. The ice island should not break up — it weighs about one billion tonnes and is bigger than anything else around it. And freshwater ice is stronger than saltwater ice. From Prince Patrick Island into the Beaufort Sea, the ice island would be moving all year, and it could be occupied throughout that time. Because of the expense of transporting accommodations and equipment, a camp that travels around for free is a very cost-efficient camp indeed.

The Polar Shelf tradition of combining dinner with planning continues. Diners are Al Singh, helicopter engineer, Larry Sobczak, geophysicist, John Currie, helicopter pilot, and George Hobson.

To study the Arctic Ocean basin, PCSP has chosen an ice island and settled in, they hope, for the next 20 years. But settling in is complicated. Field staff must keep track of its exact position, construct accommodation for dozens of scientists, pilots and technicians, and build a runway every year long and smooth enough for a Hercules aircraft to land with big pieces of equipment. In spite of the Polar Continental Shelf Project's experience in the Arctic, there is much to be learned.

Ice islands are erratic, and until now no one has deemed it necessary to track one on a daily basis. The scientists' watch began in the spring of 1982 when, in George Hobson's words, "We knew that there was a big crack in the Ward Hunt Ice Shelf and something was going to happen." In April 1983 the ice island had gone. Later that year, it was found off the mouth of Yelverton Inlet. A smaller ice chunk, which had calved at the same time and was floating just to the north of the island, was marked with empty gas drums because fog prevented a landing on the bigger island.

That was the beginning of the island watch. The island was to become a transportation vehicle for an entire camp and a runway, but

"... you don't navigate it, you don't put a motor on it. How do you keep track of it? Satellite navigation (SATNAV) and sometimes the even more accurate Global Positioning System will allow us to keep track of where it is on the globe to within a few metres. If we put detectors at two ends of the island, we can keep track of the orientation. All of this is computerized and automated, so we know where we are in real time."
— *George Hobson*

Satellite navigation is very important when men, women and equipment are floating around an unknown ocean somewhere at the top of the world. As it orbits, a satellite transmits a predetermined radio frequency. The receiver on the ice island picks up the satellite's true frequency only when the satellite is directly overhead so that when the signal is received the position of the receiver can be determined.

From Yelverton in 1983, the ice island moved to a point off Nansen Sound in 1984, and from 1983 until now, no ice island has been so closely watched.

George Hobson and Ruth Jackson, senior scientist on the refraction seismic experiments, discuss operational problems.

Where could we put the fuel bladders? We had to keep them on level ground so they wouldn't slide off during the melt. Bloop, bloop, bloop, just like that. We didn't put them out in 1985. We put the fuel in drums and carted the drums back out again.
— *George Hobson*

Richard Rondeau, helicopter mechanic, has been up all night changing a transmission so the helicopter can fly the next day.

Jay Ardai, veteran of ice island T3, John Jacobsen, technician, and George Hobson discuss where to put the big rubber fuel bladders.

They're a different breed of people. They'll do repairs on a helicopter at 45 below.
— *George Hobson*

Ruth Jackson and other scientists and technicians try to find ways of getting the most from the last aircraft hours they have allotted to them, in order to complete their experiments after many time-consuming equipment failures.

On the sea ice near the ice island, scientists drill holes for the explosives used in refraction studies in 1985. The red flag allows pilots to spot the scientists from the air; the SATNAV receiver on the tripod informs scientists of their exact position on the globe.

The ice island from the air, showing corrugations.

Once you've seen an ice island, you can spot it for miles. The biggest piece of property we have right now is the ice island. — George Hobson

Flooding the runway.

The ice island main camp, with the mountains of Ellesmere Island in the background.

Scientists and technicians unload the 1350 kg boilers used to make the holes for oceanography studies.

A helicopter is loaded with seismometers destined for different receiver locations.

Construction workers with Arctic Resources drill a hole for the runway water supply.

The hole is being drilled to get seawater for flooding the runway.

*Preparing for refraction studies. A hole is drilled through ice
and explosives are lined up in the background.*

**All the scientific work was designed to tell us more
about the structure of the continental shelf. As the
years go by, as we move along the North American
Plate on the ice island, then we'll be able to tell more
about the geology of the Arctic Ocean basin . . . and
about the general history of the whole north of the
world. — George Hobson**

SATNAV receiver equipment is set out.

*Geophysicist Larry Sobczak on his way off the island to do
gravity studies.*

Blasting equipment is wired for refraction studies.

Every time they set off a charge, I'd see the explosion, then feel the ice rise and fall under my feet. I couldn't get used to it. — Michael Foster

Dave Forsyth sets off the explosives for refraction studies.

"In 1985 it started down the coast in the manner in which it was supposed to move, and then in late August it started moving in a northeasterly direction. It returned to a point within 20 km of where it started. It has to be the wind. There were a lot of south-westerly winds. Is this normal? You look at the T3 tracks and it appears not to do that. But we weren't mark-ing T3 then and keeping track of it, and we don't really know what it did. It wasn't off in the pack ice all the time. In September and October 1985 our ice island moved back down the coast in a southwesterly direction and, at the end of 1985, it was locked in the ice at approximately 81°N, 97°W."

— *George Hobson*

There is more than enough work to be done, wherever the ice island decides to go. For Polar Shelf, the important thing is to keep the camp and runway ready and functioning smoothly. Hobson and PCSP personnel visited the island in March and again in Sep-tember 1984, to decide where to put the camp and runway. In winter the island's troughs can be so full of snow that it is hard to know where the ridges end and the troughs begin, or how deep the troughs are, or what will be under water or slide off the ridges

when the summer melt season comes. Until scientists had been there for a melt season, no one could be sure.

"In September '84 we put up seven wooden buildings. We did seismic experiments to find out whether we had to hang hydrophones below the ice island to receive acoustic signals, or whether we could put geophones on the island's surface. We found that we could receive good seismic signals on the surface, and that small charges of explosives were adequate to give us signals from the bottom and deeper. We also experimented with methods of drilling holes through the ice — whether we could do it with a hot-water drill. A hot-water drill is a very simple method of drilling a hole through the ice. You get a steel tank, put the snow in, get an oil burner underneath that heats it, send hot water down a pipe down the hole, back up and around the system, and very soon you have a hole through the ice island."

— *George Hobson*

Ideally, 1985 should have been the year for building the necessary facili-ties. But it wasn't ideal, and in the middle of learning how to build on a floating chunk of ice, parties of scien-tists were trying to work. Airplanes and helicopters were landing on and taking off from a runway that was itself experimental. With a hot-water

drill the oceanographers drilled a hole through the ice 2 m in diameter and 45 m deep. But the boilers for the drill weighed 1361 kg each, and had to be taken off a DC-3 and moved to the oceanography building by hand.

Building a 1524 m runway with nothing but PCSP resources takes time, and meanwhile a Caterpillar tractor was needed, so . . .

"somebody proposes walking the Cats down Nansen Sound and you know that every year there's a shore lead [strip of open water] and how do you get across it? They say, 'We'll just have to take that chance, George.' But I'm going to have to pay. Then, you haven't got a Hercules runway yet, so you can't fly a D4 Cat in there. So can you cut a D4 Cat apart, put it on a DC-3 airplane and fly it in on skis? Yes, you can do that, but it's going to take at least two weeks to cut the Cat apart and you will be very lucky if they can put it back together in another two weeks.

"So then you decide you're going to go with the guy who can put a snow-blower into a DC-3 and thinks he can blow a runway. We doubt it, but we have to try it. He has himself a 1066 m runway overnight, but you can't land anything on it. Too rough."

— *George Hobson*

They decided to flood the surface of the runway with seawater and let it freeze. Immediately, three problems surfaced: drilling the hole to get to the water, pumping it up 45 m, then keeping it running.

"And then you find out that you really should have four holes drilled, all flooding at the same time with four pumps going. And you should have a spare pump. And you should have two people at each hole operating the pump. And you find out that you shouldn't be using 15 m hoses. You thought it would be nice to use 15 m lengths wherever you want, but you find out that every metal coupling freezes, until you can't get a pencil through that 5-centimetre hole. And it only takes minutes to freeze."
— *George Hobson*

Nevertheless, PCSP built their 1066 m runway, and erected twelve wooden buildings and four Parcolls (large canvas and nylon structures). The camp comprised six sleeping cabins, a generator building, a navi-gation building, an office, a workshop, a kitchen-dining hall and an oceano-graphic workshop and sampling room, plus the four Parcolls as workshops and storage areas.

Through it all, the scientists worked. Hobson: "Get the bloody job done. That's my whole attitude in Polar Shelf — get the science done while you're there."

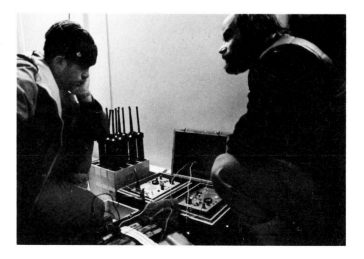

Seismologist Dave Forsyth, geophysicist Ruth Jackson, seismologist Isa Asudeh, arctic engineer Jay Ardai, electronics technician Bob Schieman and geophysicist Randy Stevenson try to solve the elusive equipment malfunctions that plague the experiments. Hot water bottles are packed with some instruments to keep them from getting too cold.

During April 1985 refraction seismic experiments were done. A chain of explosives was lowered through the ice, while recording instruments were set to record the shocks at timed intervals. Below the ice island, the energy released by the explosives penetrated layers of earth on the ocean floor. The energy was refracted back to the surface, where it was recorded. The type of material in which the energy had been refracted affected the amount of refraction and velocity.

If scientists plot the arrival time against the distance the energy has traveled, they can deduce the type of rock on the ocean floor, how far down the shocks travel to the refracting layers, and even the slope of the refracting surfaces. This provides information about the structure of the continental plate as it disappears into the Arctic Ocean.

Later in the summer, during reflection seismic studies, shocks were set off every time the island moved one kilometre. Changes in the reflected waves, as recorded at the surface, indicated the thickness, stratification and structure of the geological layers of rock beneath the track of the island.

Geological sampling was continuous, catching grab samples of bottom sediments, dredging for any bedrock outcrops, and determining the stratification of the top 122 to 152 m of bottom material. Geologists also took piston cores of the ocean floor, 100 to 160 m below the ice island, to pull up a core of 3 to 6 m of bottom material that geologists could actually look at.

Oceanographers collected water samples, and concentrated on the materials moving off the continental shelf, in the water, out into the Arctic Ocean.

The same type of scientific work has been going on since PCSP began, getting more sophisticated as the fund of knowledge increases, all designed to discover the true North, "the general history of the whole north of the world." Do we know enough? Not yet. Bill Hutchison, Assistant Deputy Minister for Earth Sciences at EMR, queries:

"Is there continuity between the Alpha Ridge, as it sticks out into the Arctic Ocean, and North America? There is a

Dave Forsyth and technicians set up and set off under-ice explosions for refraction seismic studies. These were carried out on sea ice, off the ice island.

trough between northern Ellesmere and the Alpha Ridge, but some of the material found on the Alpha Ridge is very similar to the volcanic rock on the north end of Ellesmere. If there is continuity, then the Alpha Ridge is part of North America. And if it is part of North America, then it belongs to Canada. So there is that fundamental sovereignty question. But we need more information, and time to study it."

— *Bill Hutchison*

The ice island is a continuation of the Polar Continental Shelf Project's creative method of getting the scientific job done, and it was only one of some 235 different projects throughout the Arctic in 1985. But it was the biggest one, and perhaps, 20 years from now, it will be seen to be the culmination. The island is a new learning experience for Polar Shelf. Every year the runway has to be rebuilt. Every summer it melts. Hobson would like to dam off the lakes that accumulate in the troughs in summer, so that, in September, they can pump that water up to flood the new runway for winter and spring of the next year.

For the Polar Continental Shelf Project and the scientists it supports, all challenges become opportunities.

John Currie, helicopter pilot, comes into camp.

Oh, it was wonderful heading back to Resolute with a load of empty drums. At 8 or 10 thousand feet, both ends of the drum will pop out, so you've got bang . . . bang, and there were thirty or forty drums on that flight, going bang, bang. Once they've all gone bang, bang, then you can go to sleep.
— *George Hobson*

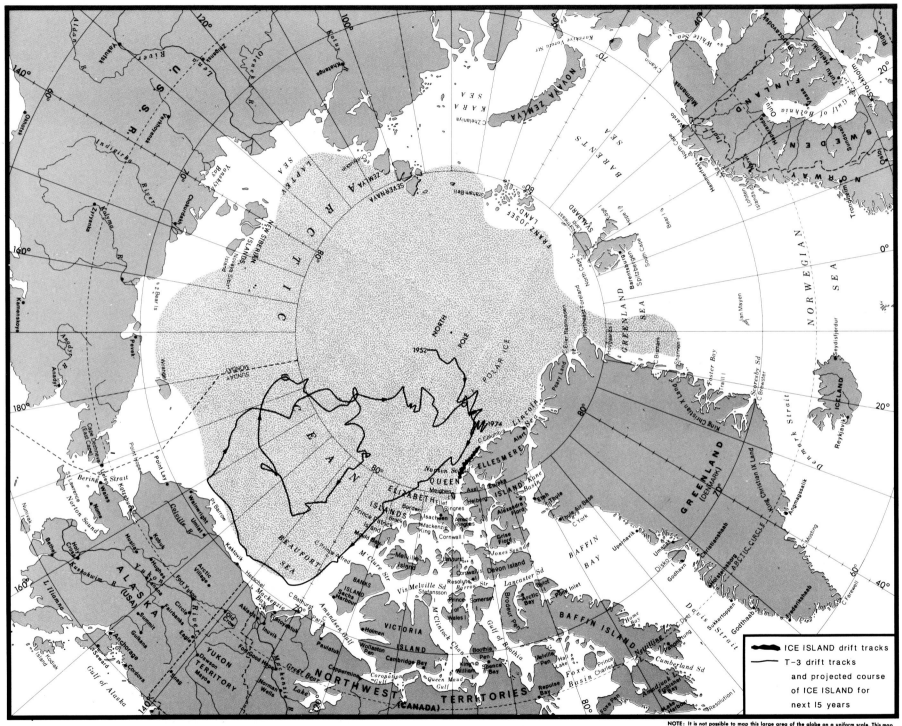

ICE ISLAND drift tracks

T-3 drift tracks
and projected course
of ICE ISLAND for
next 15 years

NOTE: It is not possible to map this large area of the globe on a uniform scale. This map is drawn on a Polar Equidistant Projection, which means that the scale along the meridians is constant but the scale in other directions varies.